WAYNE GRETZKY

The Authorized Pictorial Biography

Author, Jim Taylor

Foreword, Wayne Gretzky

WHITECAP
BOOKS

A WHITECAP/OPUS BOOK

The memories tumble out of Walter Gretzky's family archives. A pair of Peewee skates, a scrapbook, a photo album, letters and snapshots — all proud mementos of the coming of age of Wayne Gretzky.

Published and produced by Opus Productions Inc., 300 West Hastings Street, Vancouver, British Columbia, Canada V6B 1K6

This edition published in Canada by Whitecap Books Ltd., 351 Lynn Avenue, North Vancouver, British Columbia, Canada V7J 2C4

Whitecap Books (Toronto) Ltd., 602 Richmond Street West, Toronto, Ontario, Canada M5V 1Y9

First Published in 1994

10 9 8 7 6 5 4 3 2 1

Canadian Cataloguing in Publication Data
Taylor, Jim, 1937-
        Wayne Gretzky: the authorized pictorial biography

        Includes bibliographical references and index.
        ISBN 1-55110-263-3

  1. Gretzky, Wayne, 1961- –Pictorial works. 2. Hockey
players–Canada–Biography–Pictorial works. I. Title
GV848.5.G78T39 1994   796.962'092   C94-910491-4

Design: Dave Mason & Associates Inc.

Printed and bound in Canada
by DW Friesen Ltd.

*Artistic impressions — Gretzky has been the subject of
many great artists, portrayed here by Andy Warhol.*

To say that I'm very excited with the completion of this pictorial book would be an understatement! The photographs that have been selected provide a superb panavision of my life, my career and my very good fortune over the past 33 years.

When we were reviewing the thousands of possible shots to be included in the book, it made me realize how quickly time has flown by since I played my first professional hockey game. Many of the photos in this book brought back an enormous swell of warmth, pride, happiness and satisfaction when I looked at them. One or two others evoked a sadness, or sense of "if it only could have been ..." Such is life – and the people of Opus have gone above and beyond to vividly provide you with a true picture of my life.

I am sure when my children look at this book with their own children, their kids' thoughts will first and foremost be "I'm sure glad grandpa made this book!" I know I'll be forever grateful that Walter always had his camera along!

A first review of the book will tell you that not much, if anything, has been overlooked in the selection of photographs. With each following review, I hope you'll also see what has become so very evident to me. That being, when all is said and done, everything starts and ends with family.

Wayne Gretzky

November 1963. A small blond boy, all but lost in leggings, snow pants and jacket, bounces impatiently at the farmhouse door. Only his eyes are visible between his toque and the scarf wrapped around his face in anticipation of the biting winter wind.

On his feet, his first pair of skates. In his hand, a carved-down hockey stick. In a minute, his dad is going to

take him for his very first skate, right out there on the Nith River below Grandma and Grandpa's farm.

They trudge down the hill and on to the ice, the boy's arms waving in his battle to stay upright. The air is filled with laughter and shouts of encouragement as he falls, struggles upright and falls again, every move recorded on his dad's old movie camera.

Soon, they'll go back up the hill and drink hot chocolate. And when the chilblains hit his toes, his dad will take them in his hands and make the cold go away.

For Wayne Gretzky, the great adventure has begun. In two months, he will be three years old.

CHAPTER ONE

A LONG WAY FROM THE RIVER

It's

impossible, of course,

Facing page: Two years before he was technically eligible to play – and already a two-year vet – eight-year-old Wayne wears the A as Brantford's alternate captain.
Above: *Who knew they'd make history? Two-year-old Wayne Gretzky's first skates, 1963.*

but then you could say that about so much of his life: sometimes, sitting on the deck of his big house in Los Angeles, he can stare out over the swimming pool and see a river thousands of miles away, outside a town named Canning (once Mudge Hollow) just down the road from Paris – the little one in Ontario, not the big one in France.

The Nith. Hardly one of your big rivers. Big enough, though, so that a small boy could swim and paddle and fish throughout the endless summers of childhood there on his grandparents' farm. Big enough in the wondrous winters for a toddler to take those first, uncertain steps on the skates that would carry him to the top of the world. Big enough, later, for a 19-year-old to find refuge when the cost of that trip seemed far too high.

It was all getting to him then: the demands of super-stardom, the fishbowl existence, the way slices of his time were cut away so rapidly by other people that it sometimes seemed the slices added up to more than the whole, with never a portion left for him. "You know what's best?" Wayne Gretzky said once. "I can go out there to my grandma's farm and sit on the riverbank for a couple of hours, all by myself, and nobody asks me for anything."

Once he turned down $10,000 to fly from Brantford to Vancouver, say a few words at a banquet and fly home. By then the big money was starting to come in, but $10,000 was still a fair chunk. "I'd rather stay home and watch my little brother play baseball," he said, politely. On the other end of the phone, the man was baffled. But then, he didn't live in the fishbowl.

The Nith. Canning. Paris. And Brantford, Ontario, (Pop: 74,800) and the house on Varadi Avenue, with the backyard ice rink that was to become a thing of legend – "Wally Coliseum," the rink Walter Gretzky built when he grew weary of freezing beside public rinks while his son pleaded for just one more circuit, or minute, or hour.

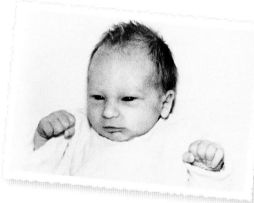

Walter and Phyllis Gretzky are proud to announce the arrival of Wayne Douglas Gretzky. Born Brantford, Ontario, January 26, 1961, 6 pounds, 8 ounces.

The rink is gone now, and maybe it shouldn't be. Maybe, like Foster Hewitt's gondola in the rafters of Maple Leaf Gardens – ripped out by Toronto Maple Leafs owner Harold Ballard in the summer of 1979 without a thought for the history it represented – it should have been preserved as a special slice of Canadiana. Wouldn't it have been interesting if the people planning the Hockey Hall of Fame could have figured a way to re-create it, as they did with the Montreal Canadiens' dressing room? Imagine

a life-sized replica of the Gretzky backyard, with the light strung on a wire from the neighbours' garage for night games and the plastic Javex bleach containers Wally set out as pylons for the skating and agility drills, and the kitchen window through which Phyllis and Walter could keep an eye on their kids until it was time to order them in and ease the chilblain pains while the circulation returned to frozen toes.

But the Gretzkys were not shrine people. As much as it is possible when strangers knock on your door and tell you they've driven all the way from the Maritimes to see Wayne's trophy room and so could you please give them a guided tour of your basement, or they go through your garbage, or rip out squares of your lawn for souvenirs, Phyllis and Walter remained as they were: bedrock people with bedrock standards passed on to all the kids.

Nor would it have occurred to Wayne Gretzky that the rink might belong as much to a country as to his family. The kids were grown, and so when he and his wife, Janet Jones Gretzky, wanted to give his parents a present, they ordered a swimming pool for the backyard on Varadi Avenue. August 9, 1988 – the date that the bulldozers began to rip out the soil that Walter Gretzky had iced over for so many winters – was significant for another reason: it was the day Wayne was traded to the Los Angeles Kings.

*If Walter Gretzky was the drive behind
the Gretzky games, Phyllis was the anchor at home,
making sure there was time for the everyday
business of family and togetherness.*

Seven-year-old Wayne at "Wally Coliseum,"
42 Varadi Avenue, Brantford, Ontario.

At 42 Varadi, games and seasons were measured in time and shoelaces. There was never enough of either. Wayne and his brothers, Keith, Glen and Brent, lived in skates and baseball shoes. Their sister, Kim, figure skated and ran track. The neighbourhood kids used "Wally Coliseum" as a second home. The family shoes never had a chance. A lace would break and the kids would dive for the closet. When they'd used them all, including the black ones in Walter's dress shoes, they'd race next door to the Rizzettos' and "borrow" some of theirs.

Forty-two Varadi was and remains a typical house on a typical street in a typical small Canadian town. If it weren't for the famous street number, tourists would drive right past. Walter and Phyllis bought the house when Wayne was eight months old: three bedrooms, living room, dining room, kitchen and basement. As the family grew, they did the usual bedroom shuffle: one bedroom for Walter and Phyllis, one for Kim, an eight-by-six for Wayne, Keith and Glen. When Brent was born, he slept in his parents' room. Later, with Wayne away so much, he got to bunk with Keith and Glen.

In 1982 the house was converted to a split-level, primarily to fight off Wayne, who wanted to buy his parents bigger, fancier digs. That added two bedrooms and gave Walter an office and storage room. In 1994 the basement was remodelled to reorganize the bulging trophy room. Otherwise, it remains the house it was when all the kids were at home and bedlam was king.

You stepped through the front door at your peril in those days, picking your way through equipment bags, hockey sticks, baseball bats, lacrosse sticks, skates, shoes – "If they could carry it, they could drop it," sighs Walter. "And what they didn't drop, their friends did." Early in the game, Phyllis gave up washing or waxing the kitchen floor in winter. The skate blades chipped the wax away, and the floor was washed by the trailed-in snow.

"When we played hockey in the backyard, we did it like the real thing," Brian Rizzetto says. "We'd stand at attention like for the national anthem, then we'd drop our gloves and wrestle. Wayne never won. But then we'd start playing hockey – showdown, three-on-one, everything. When we picked teams, Wayne always took the little guys. They won a lot. If there weren't enough kids for teams, it was practice time."

Next-door neighbour and goaltender, Rizzetto spent his winters as part of the "Coliseum" mob, operating with leverage none of the other kids possessed: the light on the Rizzettos' garage lit half the ice surface.

"I'd be in goal and if Wayne wanted to try a backhand move, he'd have me in the net for an hour, just practising it. Finally I'd say, 'I'm going home, and I'm gonna turn off the lights.' If I did that, he'd lose the half of the ice that the light from our garage covered. I'd do it, and he'd be behind me, yelling at my dad: 'Mr. Rizzetto! Brian turned the lights out! Can I get them back on?' And my dad would always say yes, and I'd be back in the nets."

When they weren't in the backyard, they were in Rizzettos' driveway, which was wider than Gretzkys'. Besides, Wally's was never shovelled. "He was too busy flooding the backyard to keep the rink going," says Mary Rizzetto. "Priorities." Brian remembers broken toes, separated shoulders and "I've got a scar on my back from one day when we were wrestling around and Wayne shoved me through a window." Windows always were a problem at 40 and 42 Varadi Avenue. They broke so many in Sylvano Rizzetto's garage that he finally gave up and put in plastic.

"I didn't flood the backyard to build a hockey star.
I flooded it so I could watch from the kitchen,
where it was warm."

WALTER GRETZKY

Hockey in the winter, lacrosse and baseball in the summer, weekend road trips to arenas around the province – it should have been paradise, and in many ways it was. There was only one problem. The little blond boy was getting too good at his games.

"He came to the tryout with his father," remembers Dick Martin, his first coach, "and here was this scared little boy. That's what he looked like – a scared little boy, trying to make a team of 10-year-olds. But I noticed something: he lost all that fright if you dropped the puck in front of him. As soon as he got that, he wasn't frightened anymore."

Maybe he should have been. In that fall of 1967, body contact was allowed in minor hockey. As the six-year-old Wayne Gretzky nervously skated onto the ice for his first tryout, he immediately disappeared into a forest of older boys. He'd be spotting four years and a lot of pounds. Besides, the whole thing was illegal. To play minor hockey you had to be 10. But he'd been on skates for four years, bugging his father for a year about playing on a real team the way they did on television, and kid-sport watchdogs hadn't yet made it to Brantford, where a half-dozen people ran the whole program.

So there he was, the future "Great One," skating around like a chihuahua in a field of dobermans, trying to win a spot on the Nadrofsky Steelers.

"I picked him because he handled the puck so well," Martin says. "He handled it at six better than my 10-year-olds. I just thought he had the ability and deserved the chance. He wasn't a good student

Nine-year-old Gretzky's oversized Steelers sweater.

of the game, not then. Remember, I was talking to 10-year-olds. If I talked down to his level they wouldn't listen, and if I talked to them I was going over his head. He was polite, always listened intently, but you could tell I wasn't getting through. The big thing was, he had Wally at home, and for teaching young hockey players there was nobody better.

"And there was this one other thing: when he had the puck, he owned it."

He was to own it for the next eight years. The numbers are staggering.

That first season he scored only one goal. (Maybe trainer Bob Phillips knew something. He fished out the puck and handed it to him. "You'll score a lot more than this," he said, "but here's the first one.") In his second season he scored 27; in his third, 104, with 63 assists in 62 games.

It was right about then that the doubters began to surface. No matter what he accomplished in one season, they assured themselves that he'd never do it again. Not against the competition he'd be looking at this year, boy. Every year, he stuck it in their ear.

As a nine- and 10-year-old in 1970-71, he scored 196 goals in 76 games and assisted on 120. "He'll never do that again," they said. They were right. Playing in 82 games (two 15-minute stop-time periods and 10 more minutes with no time stoppages), he scored 378. He was still the little guy playing one or two years ahead of his age group. But now the competition was getting stiffer. In his last three years of minor hockey the goal totals were 105, 192 and 90, lower but still the league highs.

Media attention built, year by year. In the summer following his 196-goal season, he played both baseball and lacrosse – pitching in both the house and inter-county baseball leagues and scoring 158 goals, with 66 set-ups, in 31 games for the Brantford PUC team in the inter-city lacrosse league. When the summer sports were over it was time for hockey again. Even the big city papers were wondering now: who is this kid – Superboy?

No. He was an ordinary little boy with extraordinary talents playing a schedule that would make an NHLer wince. In the 378-goal year, NHL teams played a 78-game schedule plus playoffs. Gretzky played 82. Team record: 76 wins, two losses, four ties.

"We had him and Greg Stefan carded with two teams, which you could do in those days," says Bob Hockin, his uncle and coach. "When Wayne was nine, Wally had the novice team, the Steelers, and I had the minor novice team, the Whitehorse Mustangs. Wayne played for the Steelers, but because he was only nine he could also play a year below, for me. The understanding was that the only time we used him was for tournaments."

Things could get hectic. Sometimes Wally and Bob would be on the phone at 2 a.m., phoning neighbouring towns, looking for games and ice time. Between practices and games, the Steelers were on the ice four or five nights a week. Teams elbowed each other for games in Brantford, because they earned return games at home. With the little Gretzky kid scoring all those goals, that meant a sellout.

For "The White Tornado," life should have been perfect. But he soon found out that being exceptional even in a child's league carried a heavy adult price tag. Once he came to dominate the Atom division, Brantford had a new secondary industry. If the Bell Telephone Company filled many of the local stomachs, Gretzky-watching filled their minds. Not all of the thoughts were pretty.

The first-year barbs were for Walter. What kind of father would throw a kid that little in against 10-year-olds? What was he, some kind of egomaniac? Three years later, when the puny little kid was making the 10-year-olds look silly and scoring goals at an unheard-of rate, he was deemed big enough to share the adult invective.

First trophy of many;
Wally Bauer Trophy for seven-year-old
Wayne Gretzky, Most Improved
Novice All-Star, 1968-69.

"It was there, the resentment," admits Dick Martin, who watched his climb through the divisions. "Probably not widespread, but it didn't have to be. All it took was a few parents at any one game. See, Wayne was so good that you could have a boy of your own who was a tremendous hockey player, and he'd get overlooked because of what the Gretzky kid was doing. One year Len Hachborn (who spent three NHL seasons with Philadelphia and Los Angeles) scored 100 goals. Now, 100 is a lot of goals, but he barely got mentioned, because that was the year Wayne scored 378."

"We're talking maybe a dozen people at most," says Ted Beare, longtime sports columnist with the *Brantford Expositor*. "Maybe the dozen might change as players left the team and new players and parents came along, but it wasn't a general attitude. People would say things loudly enough so Phyllis and Wally could hear them. They'd do it deliberately. That was the way they vented their anger."

Ice time was the issue and Walter Gretzky could never understand the problem. Wayne played defence – in his case, the Bobby Orr, Paul Coffey offensive defence. So did all the Gretzky boys, at first. "You learn the game better," Wally said. "You can see the whole play developing as it's coming at you, and as it's going to the other end."

> *"Wayne was so good that you could have a boy of your own who was a tremendous hockey player, and he'd get overlooked because of what the Gretzky kid was doing."*
>
> **DICK MARTIN**

As a defenceman, he got on the ice every second shift. He played the power play and killed penalties because there was no one better at it. Sometimes, when the game was in jeopardy, he'd be double-shifted at centre on the third line in the same manner other coaches used their best offensive players.

To the disgruntled Brantford parents, it didn't wash. They took stopwatches to games, clocking his total time, the length of his shifts, even how long he carried the puck at a stretch. They made notes comparing his shift times with their sons' and waved them under the coach's nose as the game ended. When Gretzky was 10, two fathers called a meeting and tried to have coach Bob Hockin replaced because he was playing Gretzky too much. "Is your nephew ever coming off?" they'd yell. Sometimes they would phone him the night before games, demanding to know how much he planned to use the Gretzky kid.

There was no escaping it, no off-season where the heat could shift to some other little kid who excelled at some other sport. There wasn't a game he didn't try or couldn't play, and when he played he dominated. In Brantford today you can still get arguments that he was a better baseball pitcher than a hockey player. Walter says his best game might have been lacrosse. Sooner or later, in every sport, the parents from hell would find him.

A rival coach in a baseball tournament sauntered up before a game. "You won't live to see Christmas, Gretzky!" he snapped. A woman who had cheered him as he set her son up for six goals in a lacrosse game was back to jeer the next night when he scored nine. He'd skipped a baseball game to play lacrosse. He was sitting with his friends, celebrating the win with a pop. It was the perfect spot to sink the knife. "Wayne, you should have gone to the baseball game," she said.

He ran home, locked the bedroom door and cried all night. What did these people want from him? He just wanted to play. The kids never gave him a bad time. Why were they doing this to him?

Walter Gretzky had his own theory. "Wayne was four feet four inches tall," he said. "They were trying to cut him down to their size."

He never answered back. Never. If he cried, it was inside, or in private. Walter might fume and snap back. Phyllis Gretzky, who would sit in another part of the stands out of earshot, would file the names away, a mental hit list to be recalled later – maybe years later – when those same people offered words of praise for the latest feats of "our" 99 and found themselves cut dead. "I get mad," Walter Gretzky said. "Phyllis gets even."

Not Wayne. In a sense, his upbringing was against him. He wasn't equipped to swap insults, snap back or do any of the things that might have silenced the abrasive minority. Adults were to be called Mr. or Mrs. (In his early years as a pro, reporters would shake their heads and suggest that, since they were meeting every day of the season, maybe he could use their first names?) The Gretzky kids learned early: if there was something worse than being a smart-mouthed kid, Wally and Phyllis hadn't heard of it.

He didn't talk that much anyway. At least, not in the presence of adults. If you talked, they might think you were showing off.

> *"If it had a ball in it, Wayne could play it, and usually better than anyone else."*
> **BRIAN RIZZETTO**

There wasn't a game he didn't try or couldn't play, and when he played he dominated. In Brantford today you can still get arguments that he was a better baseball pitcher than a hockey player. Walter says his best game might have been lacrosse.

Away from the pressures of his own sports excellence,
Wayne Gretzky had a refuge: Grandpa Tony and Grandma
Mary Gretzky's farm, where a kid could fish, swim,
drive a tractor and feed the chickens, and a young
superstar could be just plain Wayne.

So there he was, a shy, soft-spoken boy whose ability to see and hear everything in an ice rink would soon become part of NHL folklore, taking it all in and never letting anything out. Mary Rizzetto recalls this conversation:

"How'd you do today, Wayne?"

"We won."

"Score any goals?"

"Yes."

"How many?"

"Ten."

"Us kids didn't think unless we had a piece of sporting equipment in our hands," says Brian Rizzetto. "But he never mentioned playing pro some day, never lorded it over anyone. I remember a game we won 14-1 and he got 11. Same old story: somebody asked how we'd done and he said, 'We won.'

"A lot of people who resented him most kissed up to him. I got into a few fights over it. Wayne's problem was that he wasn't a fighter. He didn't try to stop it, he just walked away."

The early lessons spilled over into adulthood. One part of turning pro was easy: he had faced microphones and cameras and notebooks all his life. You said nothing that could hurt or insult or cause controversy. Another lesson from his

dad, drilled in from the day it became apparent that he might have special gifts: stardom carries responsibility. Like it or not, you're going to be an example. Years before the term was invented, Wayne Gretzky was politically correct. So he took it in silence. Besides, when it got too tough, there was always his Getaway Place – and his grandma.

Gretzky's stardom has made Mary Gretzky famous as "Grannie Goalie," the old lady who would sit in the big chair in the farmhouse living room letting her two-year-old grandson fire rubber balls off her shins with his tiny souvenir hockey stick while they watched her beloved Toronto Maple Leafs on *Hockey Night in Canada*. All true, but it doesn't begin to do her justice. The roots of the 99 work ethic were sunk in the soil of the farm on the Nith, nurtured by the lifelong example of Mary and Tony Gretzky.

Tony Gretzky was a White Russian (a native of Belorussia) who emigrated with his family to the United States a few years before

Some of the trophies were almost as big as the kid who was winning them. "If this keeps up," said Walter Gretzky, "we'll have to knock out a wall."

World War I. He crossed the border from Chicago to enlist because the Canadian army was said to have a better chance at overseas duty, served in the European theatre for the duration, then returned to Canada. With $1,500 borrowed under the War Veterans Act, he bought 25 acres with the Nith running through it. His roots were in farming. Here he would stay.

They raised cucumbers, potatoes and other vegetables, which Tony would load into sacks and carry into town. And they raised children: Sophie, Eddie, Jennie, Albert, Ellen and Walter. Then, Gretzky grandchildren ran, swam, skated, canoed and rushed pellmell through childhood there on the Nith. Wayne's first high-jump bar was the wire fence surrounding the chickens. Later, he dug long- and high-jump pits, going into the forest to cut the bar.

Pick-up "baseball" games in the farmyard – tennis racquet for a bat, tennis ball, jackets for bases, over the clothesline is out, and heaven help anyone who hits it into Grandma's garden – were played into adulthood. In 1983, with visitors in town for the Gretzky Celebrity Tennis Tournament, one game included Wayne, Keith, Brent, Glen, Detroit goalkeeper Eddie

Mio, songwriter David Foster and NFL place-kicker Eddie Murray, all throwing themselves into the dirt with an abandon that would have tested the hearts of at least three general managers and a host of music publishers.

When Tony Gretzky died in 1973, Mary spurned suggestions that she move into town and stayed on at the farm, working daily at her garden and caring for Ellen, who had been born with Down's Syndrome. When she herself contracted leukemia, she bowed her shoulders and ignored it for 13 years.

In later years it became a ritual: Mary would have an attack and be taken to hospital. Walter and the doctors would insist that she take it easy and leave the garden to someone else because the exertion was bad for her heart. Mary would

nod in agreement. The next day Walter would drive out to the farm and find her digging out weeds. "They choke my tomatoes," she'd say. End of discussion.

A determined lady, Mary Gretzky, with a firm grip on what was right and what was wrong. Right was nine-year-old Wayne playing against the Kitchener Krauts and a future NHL defenceman named Paul Reinhart in a Major Atom playoff game in Brantford Arena. Wrong was Reinhart, pinning Wayne into the boards right there in front of her. "You leave him alone!" she yelled, and belted him with her purse.

"I keep telling people that story," Reinhart said years later. "Nobody ever believes me." If they had known Mary Gretzky, they'd have understood.

When television came to the farmhouse on the Nith, she became a huge fan of Frank Mahovlich, the Maple Leafs and *All-Star Wrestling*. When Wayne turned pro, it required a quantum loyalty leap, but Grannie Goalie made it with a vengeance. There were so many pictures of Wayne on the farmhouse walls that Walter would come out when company was due and put some of them back into storage in the basement. By the time the guests got there, the pictures were back on the walls.

For all the joys of farm and family, the pressures of early stardom finally became too much. Walter Gretzky can even remember the Day of the Last Straw. February 2, 1975 – Brantford Day in Toronto's Maple Leaf Gardens, the day Brantford teams of all age levels got to play friendlies in the fabled home of the Maple Leafs with the home folks there to watch. When 14-year-old Wayne Gretzky skated out onto the ice, they booed.

Not many years later, everybody loved him. "They couldn't say enough good things about him," says sports columnist Beare. "As far as Brantford was concerned, he was the greatest thing since sliced bread. Wherever they went, they were from Wayne Gretzky's home town."

They even raised a sign proclaiming it, on the highway as you entered town: Home of Wayne Gretzky. It didn't shorten Phyllis Gretzky's list.

Autographs, interviews and fan mail: all part of a young superstar's coronation.

A WEDDING IN PARIS

In Walter Gretzky's mind there is no question as to what was the smartest move he ever made. It wasn't teaching Wayne to skate, or building "Wally Coliseum," or tucking Wayne's sweater into the side of his hockey pants. "The smartest thing I ever did," he says, "was marry Phyllis."

Walter met Phyllis Hockin in 1957 when she was 15. She knew right away that sport was going to be a priority. On dates he would take her to the rink and park her in the stands where she could watch him play Junior B hockey. "A romantic he wasn't," she says.

They married three years later. Wayne was born a year after that. Phyllis still likes to needle Walter about remembering the other kids' births by where he was at the time.

"With Kim, he dropped me off at the hospital, she was born an hour later and he took off to St. Catharines for Bell Telephone. With Keith and Glen, he was at work. But the corker was Brent: Walter was at a hockey tournament with Wayne."

Phyllis felt the baby was due. "Nah! You've got weeks yet," said the expectant father. "Come to the tournament."

Phyllis was adamant, and so they compromised. Walter and Wayne drove her to her brother Bob Hockin's house, and he drove her to the hospital while they went to the tournament. When they got back, they discovered there was a new baby.

Walter rushed to the hospital.

"It's a boy," she said.

"We won the tournament," he said.

FIVE SKATERS

Eventually there were five reasons to sit in the rink: four boys playing hockey and Kim figure skating. Winter and summer it became a juggle, because Walter and Phyllis were determined that although the hockey talent was heavily loaded in one direction, their time with their kids would not be.

If Walter watched Keith's game one night, Phyllis made certain she saw him play the next time while Walter went to watch Glen or Brent.

They would pile into the '65 Chevy, the original "Blue Goose" to make the arena runs. Walter put so many miles on it that eventually Phyllis sold it to a junk dealer for $25. That led to Goose II, bought in part with a loan from his father, Tony. Goose III, much later, was a station wagon Wayne bought his parents on a whim.

It wasn't always easy, being the sibling of the burgeoning hockey phenom. The boys heard "Aren't you Wayne's brother?" too often to count. Kim, who as the lone girl had the toughest row of all, remembers the last words of the nurse to the doctor before she slipped under the anesthetic to have her appendix removed: "Don't you recognize her? She's Wayne Gretzky's sister!"

Kim now works at the Canadian National Institute for the Blind in Brantford, Ontario. Glen is general manager of the Calgary Radz of the Roller Hockey International League. After a stint in minor pro hockey, Keith has joined the coaching ranks. Brent is playing pro hockey in the Tampa Bay Lightning organization, and has played against his famous brother.

And on June 16, 1994, at the NHL all-star awards ceremony, when Wayne was awarded with yet another Lady Byng trophy and his tenth Art Ross trophy as the league's scoring champion, the tall young man swapping jokes with actor Leslie Nielsen before they made the presentation was Brent Gretzky.

Above left: (clockwise) *Wayne, Kim, Brent, Keith and Glen.*
Above right: (left to right) *Keith, Kim, Glen and Wayne on the Blue Goose.*

PART I — ACADEMIC WORK

This refers to the subjects of study prescribed by the School program. Each is very important and a low standard of work in any one interferes seriously with normal progress.

Group I Subjects are graded by marks or letters. Because of the difficulty of assessment, Group II Subjects are graded by letters only and may be interpreted. Group II Subjects are graded by letters C, 65-74%; D, 50-64%; E, 40-49%.

A letter grading of E on group II subjects, and average marks of 59 or lower on group I subjects indicate that promotion is in danger.

GROUP I SUBJECTS	FALL TERM	WINTER TERM	SPRING TERM	FINAL RATING
Composition and Grammar (100)				
Literature and Silent Reading (100)	75	70	73 →
Mathematics (100)	74	75	76 →
Spelling (50)	75	75	80 →
Writing (50)	37	40	42 →
Social Studies (100) or History (50) + Geography (50)	32	45	45 →
Science (100)				
GROUP II SUBJECTS				
Music	77	78	80 →
Health and Phys. Ed.	76	80	82 →
Arts and Crafts	B	B	B →
Oral Reading	B	B	B →
	B	B	B →
	B	B	B →
	B	B	B →

Pupil's Average Group I Subjects _____ 74 77
Class Average Group I Subjects _____ 74 74
Teacher's Comments:
Fall Term: 79 / 75

Wayne is making good progress.

Winter Term:
Wayne is a very steady student. He is making good progress. His hockey fame has not hindered his scholastic achievement.
Spring Term:
Wayne has done very well. He is a neat worker and tries his best at all times. His achievement shows this.

Try to improve your record from month to month

PART II — CITIZENSHIP FUNDAMENTALS

These are important aspects of a child's education and are developed through such environmental factors as the home, the school program, the personnel, the conditions of the home, the kind of playmates, the spare time interests, and so forth. Proper attitudes and good work habits, teamed with one's best academic achievement, insure success.

Marking Code: S—Quite Satisfactory
P—Showing Progress
N—Improvement Needed.

WORK HABITS	FALL TERM	WINTER TERM	SPRING TERM
Neatness of Work			
Promptness in commencing and completing work	S	S	S
Persistence of effort			
SOCIAL ATTITUDES			
Courtesy	S	S	S
Consideration for property and rights of others	S	S	S
Self-control	S	S	S
HEALTH HABITS			
Personal Cleanliness	S	S	S
Posture			
Proper Rest	S	S	S
Teacher's Comments:	S	S	S

Fall Term:
Wayne has very good work habits. He is polite and well behaved.

Winter Term:
Very good!

Spring Term:
Good luck Wayne — in both your school work and sports!

—As Needs Good Citizens — Do Your Best

SCHOOL EXERCISE

NAME Wayne Gretzky
SUBJECT
SCHOOL   No. 680

MAKING THE GRADE

Bob Taylor, principal, Greenbriar Elementary School, offers this "scouting report" on Wayne Gretzky, student: *Academic potential:* Good student. Would have been outstanding scholar, but was honing other special talent.

Not a cause for worry. We always felt he would propel himself through school the way he would propel himself through athletics.

Disciplinary problems: None.

Leadership: School had exceptional athletes. One year lost only one volleyball playoff game. Everything else – basketball, baseball, track – we had the county championship. Wayne always took command, but always in a quiet way. Never authoritarian.

Attitude: Never initiated discussions about his games outside school. When asked, comments focused on team, not personal accomplishments. In school games, he'd play, then stay to help coach tidy up.

Dedication: Practised at every opportunity with team, but always wanted pre-game time to himself to get feel of field or court or ice. It was a private thing.

Summation: Came from home that cared about him as an individual and instilled values. Never worried about him as a boy.

Watching him get to where he is and handle it all has been fascinating.

Above: *Report card, exercise book and school photos – memories of Grade Three. Principal's note: "His hockey fame has not hindered his scholastic achievement."*

THE ONCE AND FUTURE KINGS

The Howe-Gretzky relationship began in a limousine on the way to the 1972 Kiwanis "Great Men of Sports" Dinner in Brantford.

The head table would include hockey-great Gordie Howe, quarterback Joe Theismann of the Toronto Argonauts, former Chicago Blackhawks coach Rudy Pilous, baseball's Sal "The Barber" Maglie, Baltimore Colts running back Tom Matte, Hamilton Tiger-Cats defensive tackle Angelo Mosca – and 11-year-old, four-foot-nine-inch, 80-pound Wayne Gretzky, who had just completed a 378-goal season.

Howe kept the conversation going.

"You practise your backhand shot?" he asked.

"Yes, sir."

"That's good. Always work on that."

"Yes, sir."

(The words must have sunk in. His first goal in Junior B, his first goal in Junior A, his first goal in the WHA and his first goal in the NHL were all on backhands. When your hero speaks, you listen.)

There was a mix-up at the banquet. Wayne wasn't supposed to speak. But he was called to the microphone and left standing, tongue-tied. There was an awkward silence. Then Howe walked to the microphone, put his arm around the blushing youngster and said, "When someone has done what this kid has done in this rink, he doesn't have to say anything."

The cement was set on a friendship that began as boy-and-hero and developed into legend-and-legend. But for Wayne, the hero-worship never went away.

Above: *44-year-old Gordie Howe meets 11-year-old Wayne Gretzky.*

*Being the littlest kid on the ice rarely bothered Gretzky,
but in 1970 he discovered the other side of hockey,
getting flattened in the zone finals.*

If he keeps going, Wayne Gretzky may some day hit the 1,000 goal mark in the NHL.
As a minor hockey player he scored No. 1,000 playing for Turkstra Lumber on
April 10, 1974. He was 13 years old.

"They seek him here, they seek him there …" but from the start,
he had a way of appearing alone in front of the net. "Hitting him,"
Glen Sather would later say, "is like trying to hit confetti."

Goal No. 100, 1971.

*Fiftieth goal in nine games at
a Hespeler, Ontario, tournament,
January 1, 1972.*

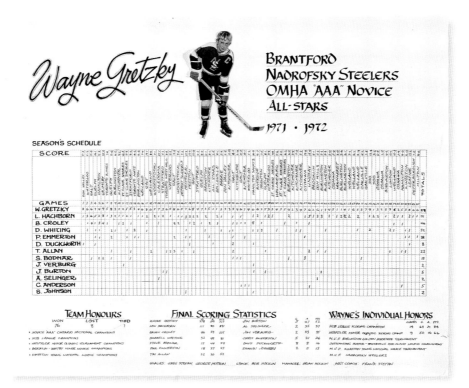

*Giant replica of a gigantic season: 82 games, 378 goals, 139 assists
for 517 points for Nadrofsky Steelers Novice All-Stars, 1971-72.*

*Goal No. 100, Goderich, Ontario,
January 21, 1973.*

*Career goal No. 700
in the final game of a
Kingston, Ontario tournament.*

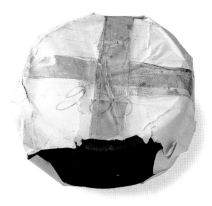

Game No. 200,
January 23, 1972, Wayne scored
seven goals against Kitchener.

Goal No. 300, 1971-72,
for the Nadrofsky Steelers.

Wayne (front centre) and Walter (back right) at
the Hespeler (Ontario) Minor Olympics, 1970-71.

Career goal No. 800,
March 10, 1973.

Goal No. 100,
January 2, 1974, 3-2 loss
to Burlington, Ontario.

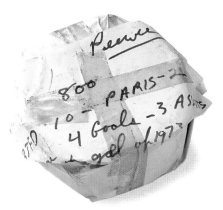

When Walter Gretzky wasn't
snapping pictures, he collected
Wayne's milestone pucks,
wrapping and labelling each
one to preserve the memories.

A TALE OF TWO CITIES

Out of his helter-skelter 1970-71 schedule came one of the young Gretzky legends: two games, two cities, one day.

He was nine. The Steelers were in a tournament in Hespeler, the Mustangs in another in Welland. Distances: Brantford to Hespeler, 15 miles. Brantford to Welland, 60 miles. Hespeler to Welland, 75 miles. With games in one tournament at night followed by a day game in the other, they had managed to get him to both. The finals would be a different story – in the morning in Welland, in the afternoon in Hespeler. It was out of the question, Bob and Walter agreed. Wayne wouldn't play the Welland final.

The next morning, a tearful nine-year-old was tugging at his dad's bedclothes. "Please, let me play in Welland," he begged. Wally poked the sleeping Phyllis. "Phone Bob in Welland. Tell him to get Wayne's name on the scoresheet so he can play when he gets there. We're on our way."

Wayne dressed while Wally drove. At the Welland arena, team manager Doug Whiting scooped Wayne out of the car, carried him in (who had time to let him walk?) and sat him on the bench. Brantford trailed 2-0. Before long, it was 5-0. Gretzky scored four goals. Brantford won 6-5. Walter raced for the parking lot, started the engine and threw open the back door. Whiting raced out, carrying Wayne, and threw him into the car. Walter gunned it for Brantford. Wayne dashed into the house to change jerseys and gulp a glass of milk. They got to Hespeler in time, Wayne starred, Brantford won.

"How was your day, Wally?" someone asked.

"Average," he sighed. "Just average."

CHAPTER TWO

For

those blessed with

Facing page: *For Gretzky, every season had to begin with a target. As he settled in with the Soo Greyhounds, his sights were set on 171 points, one more than the league's scoring leader the previous season.* Above: *In small-town Canada, nothing is bigger than Junior hockey. Greyhound fans turned out with pennants flying to see the Gretzky kid.*

the talent to make it and the luck to get the chance, the road from minor hockey to the National Hockey League is reasonably straightforward. You work your way through the minors — from Peewee to Bantam to Midget to Junior. You get drafted out of Midget by a Junior A team, play there for three or four years, get drafted by an NHL club, report to training camp, and you're on your way.

Wayne Gretzky took a slightly different route. First he went to Toronto; then to assorted provincial hockey tribunals to lose a battle with minor hockey's blazer brigade to play on a Bantam team in Toronto; then to a Junior B team; then to a Junior A team miles from home where he didn't want to be; and then to a rebel pro league, for more money than he had ever imagined, to serve as one of the major bullets in an inter-league shootout. By this time he was 17 years old.

The odyssey began because he had to get out of Brantford. He was 14, famous, envied and under a microscope. Reluctantly, the Gretzkys agreed to let him go to Toronto, live with Bill and Rita Cornish, attend school there and play his hockey as one little fish in the Young Nationals hockey organization, which operated teams in several divisions and was 10,000 players strong.

He moved, enrolled in school, made friends – and everything hit the fan. The Brantford Minor Hockey Association had agreed to the transfer. The Ontario Minor

Hockey Association did not. Despite the fact that the Gretzkys had signed a paper making the Cornishes Wayne's legal guardians, he was deemed to be breaking the residency rule.

Walter couldn't understand it. "This isn't about hockey," he said. "This is about the boy. He's not happy here. We're worried about him. Toronto's only 60 miles away. He can come home weekends. People send their kids away to boarding school and nobody says anything. What's the problem?"

Every appeal failed. He couldn't play Bantam hockey anywhere but in Brantford. "I'm not going back, Dad," he said. "Regardless, I'm not going back."

He took the only other course open. He stayed with the Cornish family and signed up with the Young Nats' Junior B team, the Vaughan Nationals, who didn't

Wayne as a Junior B Vaughan National.

come under the authority of Ontario minor hockey – 14-year-old, 135-pound Wayne Gretzky, in against 20-year-olds. When he scored two goals and killed penalties in his first game, Wally quit worrying. As the turmoil swirled around him, he finished with 27 goals and 33 assists, despite starting the season two months late, and was named rookie of the year. In his second season, after an early bout with mononucleosis, he led the club (by then called the Senecas) to the league title.

It had started out ugly, complete with rumours of bribes to Walter to get Wayne to the Nats, and stories painting him as a hockey-mad, money-hungry parent pushing his son to the NHL. But the Brantford ghosts were behind him, and hockey was fun again. The only foul-up was the part about playing where he'd never be noticed.

He was noticed, all right, by every Junior A team in Ontario. He'd been called up to Junior A for three games with the Peterborough Petes and set up three goals. Although he'd played two years of Junior B, he was at the age when he would normally have been entering his second year of Midget and was thus eligible for the Junior A draft.

> *"I'm 14 years old, playing with guys old enough to have driver's licenses and drink beer!"*
>
> **WAYNE GRETZKY**

Walter wrote to all the teams not within driving range of Brantford. He and Phyllis had had enough of the absentee parent business. The family needed to be together again. "Don't draft Wayne," he wrote. "He won't report." The Sault Ste Marie Greyhounds drafted him anyway. "It was hilarious," says Muzz MacPherson. "We called out his name and almost got killed right there in the room."

Murray "Muzz" MacPherson was to play a brief but huge role in the Gretzky saga. But at that time he was just a Junior A coach looking for talent, and Wayne was not his first pick.

"I wanted Tom McCarthy," he admits. "Our scouts had seen Wayne, knew he was a good player.

But he was still 16, and I'd seen a lot of Tom. So we go to the draft and there they are, all the team owners and coaches, swapping choices and picks from the next year's draft, making deals to get into position.

"Peterborough wanted Wayne badly, but picked fourth. They made one deal with Oshawa, which picked first, not to touch him. They made another deal with Kitchener, which picked second. We pick third – but nobody talks to us.

"Oshawa goes first, and takes McCarthy. Kitchener goes second, and takes Paul Reinhart. Now it's our turn, and Angelo Bumbacco, the general manager, stands up and says, 'The Soo Greyhounds select Wayne Gretzky!'

The Peterborough guys are across the room like a shot, screaming and calling us every name in the book. 'He won't play for you! He's told you that!' They never thought we'd take the chance, but with McCarthy gone …"

Walter was furious. Hadn't he told them? Didn't anybody listen? Still, the irony was not lost on him. "I try to move my son 60 miles down the road to Toronto and hockey says I can't," he sighed. "Now we don't want him to play 500 miles away from home and hockey says I have to. They were worried about a 14-year-old boy being away from home, but a 16-year-old boy is fine?"

They settled it as they had settled it in Toronto. Jim and Sylvia Bodnar had moved from Brantford to The Soo. Wayne had played minor hockey with their son, Steve. Wayne, who had been just as adamant as Walter about not playing there, changed his mind when he was offered a chance to live with people he knew.

"It didn't happen just like that, pow!" MacPherson says. "But we finally get it settled and figure everybody's happy. But by now Wayne's got an agent, Gus Badali, and after about the eighth meeting, just as we're coming to terms, Gus says, 'He's got to have No. 9.' Up to then the number had never been mentioned. But how can I give him No. 9? Brian Gualazzi has had it for three years. You don't take a number away from a vet to give it to a kid, I don't care who he is. But Wayne wants 9 because he's idolized Gordie Howe

"Don't draft Wayne, he won't report."

WALTER GRETZKY

Dispatch from the front.
Gretzky gets his marching orders for Junior A.

He was 16 years old, in a strange town, carrying with him a minor-hockey reputation as a worker of miracles. Now all the new Soo Greyhound had to do was prove it.

for years, and he's had it through a lot of his minor hockey."

Wayne reported to the Greyhounds with nothing settled. When they opened the season in Sudbury where they hadn't won in two years, he was wearing 19. He had three goals and three assists.

"I figure that takes care of the number thing," says Muzz. "But halfway home on the bus he comes down the aisle and says, 'You know, I really don't like this number.'

"'Yeah,' I said. 'You only got six points. It really hurt you.' But he wasn't kidding. He wanted to try another one. So for a while he wears 14, but it's obviously bugging him, and it's bugging Badali. And I'm in a bind, because Gualazzi wants to keep 9, and there's no way I'm gonna take it from him."

Then they got a break. The Boston Bruins traded Phil Esposito and Ken Hodge to the Rangers. MacPherson knew there was no way Espo was going to get his old No. 7 in New York. Not unless the Rangers traded Rod Gilbert. "Angelo! Phone Espo!" he yelled. "Find out what number he's going to wear." The answer came back: Espo was bumping from 7 to 77. Bingo!

The next day, MacPherson picked Gretzky up at school and drove him to his office. As Wayne sat down, Muzz reached out and closed the office door. "There's your new number," he said. "You can't wear one 9, wear two." Hanging on the door was a Greyhounds jersey. The number on it was 99.

"You can't wear one 9, wear two."

MUZZ MACPHERSON

"Wayne looked at me funny for a minute. Then he said, 'Muzz, guys see that, they'll be running at me all night.'"

"Wayne," said MacPherson, who had seen the 16-year-old get nine goals and 31 points in pre-season, "they're gonna run you anyway."

By his own admission, Gretzky was not exactly awestruck at the prospect of stepping into Junior A. At his first practice he asked MacPherson how many points Mike Kaszycki, the league scoring champion, had the previous season.

"One hundred and seventy," said Muzz.

"No problem," he replied. "I'll break that."

He was half right. He did break it. But Bobby Smith of Ottawa broke it better. They battled all season, and Smith finished with 69 goals and 192 points to Gretzky's 70 goals and 182 points. Third place and the goal-scoring title went to Dino Ciccarelli of the London Knights with 72 goals and 70 assists, for 142 points.

It was not a picnic season. They did run at him. In Junior B he had kidded about playing against married guys with mortgages when he couldn't even drive. Now he was winning aftershave as player of the game before he had started to shave.

"When he got there, some noses were out of joint," MacPherson admits. "There were guys who'd been there for two, three years and the spotlight had been on them. Now here was this kid, getting all the publicity. Everybody was waiting to see how good he really was, and I don't think they'd have been too upset if he flopped."

Clockwise from top left: *Life as a budding superstar. Gretzky tied the rookie
goal-scoring record at 67 (and upped it to 70), posed for the promotional shots,
got his first taste of the endless interviews that would go with being a pro*

In November, MacPherson called a meeting. Wayne was not invited. "Wayne's young," he told the Greyhounds. "He has a lot to learn, but he's a great hockey player. Some day you're gonna be proud just to be able to tell your kids and grandchildren you played with him. He's gonna set records that aren't gonna be broken for a long, long time."

MacPherson himself didn't survive the season. Gretzky's big year wasn't enough to carry a floundering team. Wayne was starring but the team was losing. Muzz resigned in February, carrying a bagful of his own memories of a superstar in the making.

"We're in Ottawa one night, losing 4-1 at the end of two periods, and we've got a game against a big, tough Hamilton club the next night. I was worried about Wayne getting too banged up, so I told him this one was over and he wouldn't be playing much in the third. He's hot. 'You think this is my fault?' he asks.

"But I sit him out until about seven minutes left. It's still 4-1, but one of their guys gets a spearing penalty and we're on the power play, so I tap Wayne on the shoulder and say go.

"He's still ticked off at being benched. 'You want me to win it, or tie it?' he says, kind of sarcastic.

One of two goals in a 7-4 loss to Oshawa – Gretzky's 100th point as a Greyhound, January 5, 1978.

"'A tie would be lovely,' I say. So he goes out and scores three goals and we get the tie. So he's coming off the ice and one of our kids looks at me.

"'You made a mistake, coach,' he says. 'You should have told him to win it.'"

As it turned out, that was Gretzky's first and last year of Junior A hockey. He had chafed under Paul Theriault, the Greyhounds' new coach, who severely cut his ice time and had him concentrating more on defence. Did he want three, maybe even four more years of a style that was putting him in hobbles? No way. There was a hockey war breaking out between the NHL and the new World Hockey Association. Maybe 17 wasn't too young to enlist.

Years later, Walter Gretzky sat back one evening and considered how things might have gone.

"If people had let him be, he'd probably have stayed in Brantford for all his minor hockey. He'd have gone to Junior A a couple of years later, done three or four years there instead of one, probably been the first or second NHL draft pick, wound up with a bad team, missed Edmonton entirely, never been a part of those great Oiler teams, never have wound up in Los Angeles. So I guess you could say it worked out."

So, in a crazy way, that tiny minority of adults who couldn't live with the success of a young boy actually made a significant contribution to the history of professional hockey in North America?

"I guess so," he conceded. "What is it they say? 'Go figure.'"

The Weekend Citizen

with
The Canadian Magazine, Color Comics, TV/Times

Home delivered 85¢ weekly.   35¢ per copy

Ottawa, Saturday, January 7, 1978

135th Year, Number 159, 206 pages

Super star showdown

— Tim O'Lett, Citizen

Wayne Gretzky (9) of Sault Ste. Marie Greyhounds and Ottawa 67's Bobby Smith had a chance to strut their stuff Friday night before 7,077 fans — the largest crowd of the season at the Civic Centre. Smith emerged as the winner with a six-point performance in helping 67's to a 9-5 victory. Gretzky was held goalless. (Details on pages 13 and 14)

CHASING RECORDS

Bobby Smith remembers Wayne Gretzky's one year with the Soo Greyhounds, and thanks him for it. Without Gretzky, Smith would not still be in the OHA Junior A record books.

Smith retired following the 1992-93 season after a fine 16-year career with the Minnesota North Stars and Montreal Canadiens. But his Junior A scoring record of 192 points in a single season still stands.

"You know what did it?" he asks. "It was the thought, every night, that that skinny little guy in The Soo was chasing me. He was relentless. If he had three points after two periods, that was never enough no matter what the score. He was always pushing for three more. I was leading the league in scoring, but he was always back there breathing down my neck, and I always knew it, so I couldn't let up, either."

Naturally, the league played up the season-long scoring race. When Ottawa played The Soo, it was Smith vs. Gretzky. "We even had penalty-shot competitions against each other, once in Ottawa, once in The Soo," Smith says. "I won in Ottawa, he won in The Soo, and I think it drew about 3,000 fans above average each night."

Smith has one more special memory of the many times he was to go against Gretzky in the NHL. "Remember the rookie year when he tied with Marcel Dionne for the scoring championship? Well, one night the Oilers were playing us in Minnesota. For some reason, the mesh on the nets in the Met Center was always loose. If you shot hard enough, sometimes the puck would go right through.

"Well, I saw Wayne score one. He cut to the left and shot across his body, and the puck went right through the mesh. It happened so fast the ref didn't see it and the Oilers didn't, either. But I had just the right angle. He scored that goal. It would have broken the tie. But nobody saw it but me."

Above: The season-long battle between Oshawa's Bobby Smith, completing his final year of Junior at 20, and the 17-year-old Soo rookie, made headlines whenever they met.

"Guys would say to me, 'Aren't you playing him too much?' Hell, what was I supposed to do? Every time I yelled, 'We need a centre out there,' he'd be over the boards and gone."

MUZZ MACPHERSON

"Wayne's young. He has a lot to learn, but he's a great hockey player. Some day you're gonna be proud just to be able to tell your kids and grandchildren you played with him. He's gonna set records that aren't gonna be broken for a long, long time."

MUZZ MACPHERSON

"Wayne Gretzky will get 'killed' if he turns professional at the age of 17. That's the opinion of Howie Meeker, the outspoken analyst of *Hockey Night in Canada*.

"Meeker was commenting on a report that Gretzky would turn pro if the World Hockey Association decided to draft underage juniors this year. 'It would retard his development,' Meeker said . 'He's still a boy. Not many 19-year-olds are ready for the pros.'

"Meeker admitted that he had only seen Gretzky play on television during the world junior championship last December. 'He's not mature physically yet,' Meeker said. 'Now I don't know his personality. I know he can outthink and outsmart the others and his skating is not that bad – I didn't see anybody catch him from behind. But turn pro at 17 – he'd get killed.'"

Brantford Expositor, May 4, 1978

In
any other year,

Facing page: *Gretzky the pro: still a kid, hockey was still a game, and the pure fun of it could come out at any time.* Above: *His first pro goal – Indianapolis Racers – October 22, 1978.*

all of Wayne Gretzky's escape hatches from junior hockey would have been closed. The NHL – the only game in town for better than half a century – wasn't about to sign kids before they graduated from Junior A. It didn't make sense to chop at the roots of the amateur tree, which provided the upcoming talent at little or no cost. You did your time and waited for the draft and the phone call telling you where you would be playing. Oh – you don't want to play there? Too bad. Next!

Things got a little better in 1971 with the formation of the World Hockey Association. In addition to going out and signing established NHL stars like Bobby Hull and Derek Sanderson for money the NHL wouldn't dream of paying, the WHA was reaching into the junior talent pool and scooping some of the bigger fish. This led to an agreement between the warring leagues that neither would sign under-agers. But in the summer of 1978, at the very moment Wayne Gretzky was fuming to get out of The Soo, John Bassett, Jr., owner of the Birmingham Bulls was saying to hell with it, he would sign anyone he pleased.

Bassett was already known as the man who fired the first shot in the NHL-WHA war by signing 18-year-old Wayne Dillon of the Toronto Marlboros in 1973 when the Bulls were the Toronto Toros. Now he had done it again, taking 18-year-old Ken Linseman from the Kingston Canadians. As soon as he read about it, Wayne was on the phone. "Call him, Dad," he said. "Call him now."

Bassett offered a one-year deal for $80,000. Gus Badali turned it down. The New England Whalers, seeing the NHL-WHA agreement falling apart, offered a $200,000 signing bonus and an eight-year deal. Wayne was excited. He'd be playing on a team with Gordie Howe. But the Whalers, figuring they had a chance to be part of any merger with the NHL and not wanting to hurt their chances by alienating any of the governors who would be doing the voting, withdrew the offer. Bassett still wanted Wayne, but was stretched thin financially.

Enter Nelson Skalbania, who was about to set the game on its ear. Skalbania was a Vancouver real-estate developer, racquetball player, runner and high-stakes backgammon player who had turned to sports franchises with a passion usually reserved for his land flips. In 1981, the high point, he owned the Atlanta Flames of the NHL, the Montreal Alouettes of the Canadian Football League, the Calgary Boomers of the North American Soccer League, junior hockey franchises in Calgary and New

Westminster, B.C., and 50 percent of the Vancouver Canadians of the Pacific Coast Baseball League. He had tried to buy the Seattle Mariners major league baseball franchise, and had a National Basketball Association franchise for Vancouver in his pocket for $20 million. (He stood by his $16-million offer, and the bid fell through). It was said he made more million-dollar deals on cocktail napkins and serviettes than a lot of people did in boardrooms. His route through hockey proved that over and over again.

In the summer of 1976, Nelson Skalbania stood at a press conference in an Edmonton restaurant, announcing that he had just purchased the WHA's Edmonton Oilers from Dr. Charles Allard, Zane Feldman and Bill Hunter. Sitting at a nearby table, enjoying a quiet dinner with his wife, was Edmonton entrepreneur Peter Pocklington.

He leaped to his feet.

"I want half!" he said. "I'll take half!"

That was okay with Skalbania. He had done a lot of previous deals with Pocklington, and in those days the less you owned of a WHA franchise, the better off you were. "Peter didn't have any ready money," he says, "but he had toys – diamonds, paintings, cars, things like that. He literally took a diamond ring off his wife's finger as she sat there at the table, and gave it to me. The rest of the deal was a Rolls-Royce convertible and a bunch of paintings."

"People always wondered what Wayne was making as a junior, since he was such a big star. I told them $25 a week. That was a lie. He was making $24.01. They took off 99 cents tax."

WALTER GRETZKY

Hockey was the road to fame and riches, but even the big contract to come didn't cool his love for baseball, or stop the pickup games at home with friends.

There they were in the WHA, a seven-team league with one of the teams – the Indianapolis Racers – in near-collapse. The Indianapolis people said they would make it easy for Skalbania if he would buy the franchise: no dollars down, just take it over and try to save it. Now he owned 50 percent of one franchise and 100 percent of another. When he saw them play each other ("Talk about watching paint dry …") he knew he had to do something.

"Sign the Gretzky kid," suggested John Bassett, Jr. With those words, he officially opened the circus.

"You know why I wanted Wayne to turn pro?" asks Gus Badali. "Because I thought he'd be safer in the pros than staying in Junior A. He'd been so dominant that first year, I was truly concerned that he wouldn't survive a second. He barely survived the first one. The number of goons taking swings at him illegally was incredible. I honestly thought he'd be safer in the WHA playing against men who didn't know much about him and wouldn't feel they were going to be big guns by beating up this kid.

"I'd seen a game in Hamilton in Junior B when he'd literally beaten the other team by himself, and two 20-year-olds pummelled him. They definitely would have been in jail if it had happened in the street. I saw it happen in Hamilton again in Junior A. They had six guys you could put in jail. I felt that in his second year, somebody would gun him down."

"Hockey is entertainment. You've got to have a star."
NELSON SKALBANIA

Badali and Skalbania met in Toronto. Badali asked for a $250,000 signing bonus. Skalbania reached into his pocket, pulled out about 10 one-hundred-dollar bills and said, "Here. I want you and the family and Wayne to fly out to Vancouver tomorrow and we'll negotiate."

Walter didn't want to go. He hated flying. And he certainly couldn't go in the middle of the week. He was a working man. They settled for the weekend. Skalbania met them in the Rolls-Royce, which broke down in the driveway of his mansion. Knowing nothing about hockey, he checked Wayne's fitness by taking him for a five-mile run. "He beat me, I think, or could have," he says.

A deal was reached that night. The next day they boarded a private jet for Edmonton. Skalbania, who still owned half the Oilers, wanted to make the announcement there. But the wording of the contract wasn't quite to Badali's satisfaction. Skalbania handed Wayne a blank piece of paper. "Here," he said. "You write it." The 17-year-old carefully took down the new wording of the deal that would make him rich: a $250,000 signing bonus and four years' salary. Total package: $825,000. Skalbania gave him a $50,000 cheque to seal the bargain, they landed in Edmonton for one press conference and then flew to Indianapolis for another.

It was not a WHA contract, or even a hockey contract. It was a personal services contract between Skalbania and Wayne, with Walter's agreement because Wayne was not of legal age. In case the Indianapolis situation didn't improve, it also had a clause under which Wayne agreed to play either there or in Houston, a franchise Skalbania had been offered under much the same terms that he had purchased the Racers.

At that time, no one was certain that the WHA would stand firm on its policy of signing under-age players. What happens, Skalbania was asked, if it turns out Wayne can't play?

"In that case," he replied, "I've just bought myself the most expensive racquetball partner in history."

In a storybook, the little kid from Brantford would go to the Racers, fill the rink and lead them on to the championship. "We landed in Indianapolis, and I made the announcement that we'd signed Wayne and were committed to keeping hockey alive in Indianapolis," says Skalbania. "Ticket sales soared from 2,100 to 2,200."

Obviously, Indianapolis was not a hockey town. The team was bleeding Skalbania to death. The way it worked out, each game cost him twice as much to stage as people were paying to see it. In eight games, Wayne had only three goals and three assists. The big experiment was a flop.

> "You get Gretzky and I'll be there before he is. If you've got him, you've got the guy who'll be the franchise."
>
> **JOHN FERGUSON**

Skalbania decided to sell him to another WHA club. He called Michael Gobuty of the Winnipeg Jets and said, "Michael, maybe you'd like to do something with Wayne." Gobuty and one of his partners promptly hopped into Gobuty's private jet, flew to

First pro stop. Eight games as an Indianapolis Racer.

Indianapolis and flew back to Winnipeg. En route, they struck the deal that would have made Gretzky a Winnipeg Jet.

"It was for a couple of players," Skalbania says. "I told him he had the option until the plane landed and we talked to his general manager, John Ferguson. Then I was going somewhere else. We landed, and the deal was nixed."

("Not by me," insists John Ferguson, now player-personnel director of the Ottawa Senators. "When I was talking to Gobuty about taking over as GM and he said there was a chance to get Gretzky, I said, 'You get Gretzky and I'll be there before he is. If you've got him, you've got the guy who'll be the franchise.' But we had scouts who said he was too small and wasn't worth the money because he'd never make it.")

Whatever. The deal fell through. Skalbania walked across the airport concourse and phoned Pocklington in Edmonton. A few weeks earlier he had done a deal with the man they'd started calling Peter Puck, selling him his half of the Oilers ("for more paintings, another Rolls-Royce – if I got any money, I don't remember"). Now he said, "You know the deal for Gretzky. It's yours if you want it." "Okay," said Peter Puck.

Winnipeg Jets had missed out on landing No. 99. A decade later, they'd get another chance.

Personal service contract between Wayne Gretzky
and N.M. Skalbania.

1) This contract to be guaranteed by N.M. Skalbania
personally.

2) There will be a 250,000.00 signing bonus, 50,000.00
of which will be recieved upon signing this
agreement and the remainder of the bonus
(200,000.00) and contract terms are to be
approved by Wayne's solicitors and are not
binding upon him until the written approval
is given.

3) The term of the contract shall be a period of
4 yrs.
(A) first yr   100,000.00 ⎤
    second yr   150,000.00 ⎬ Canadian Funds
    third yr   150,000.00 ⎦
    fourth yr   175,000.00

(B) There shall be a (3) yr option to renew this
contract by N.M Skalbania on terms to be
mutually agreed upon, and if such agreement
is not readily obtained, it shall be arbitrated
by a neutral arbitrator.

1) Wayne Gretzky, as a condition of this contract must
be prepared to work starting June 1/78 with
either Houston or Indianapolis.

(2)

(6) Wayne Gretzky, his agent, his family, etc. shall hold the WHA and the NHL and all of their agents representatives, owners etc. harmless if a merger or any other form of accomodation between the two leagues results in the negation of this contract. This contract shall be null and void if there is an accomodation between the NHL and the WHA such that it is a requirement that underage juniors do not play. In any event, all funds advanced to Wayne Gretzky up to the day of cancellation shall be retained by Wayne Gretzky as liquidated damages.

7) On Wayne's 18th birthday, he must resign new contract that is identical to the ne agreeable to Wayne's solicitors, otherwise he contract becomes null and void.

Signed Agreed.

N.M. Skalbania

N. M. SKALBANIA

WAYNE GRETSKY

Wayne Gretzky

WALTER GRETSKY

Walter Gretzky

GUS BADALI

Gus Badali

DATED

JUNE 10/78

"I looked down at that contract Wayne had just written out," Badali said. "It was maybe the biggest deal in the history of the game for a junior and bigger than most for anybody in hockey, period. I looked through the window at the storm, then over to Walter and Wayne. And I have this sudden thought:

"'Migawd, Walter,' I said. 'I've just negotiated this huge contract, and if we crash, nobody's ever going to know!"

Wayne's copy of the document that would shake professional hockey: taking dictation from Nelson Skalbania, Gretzky wrote out this personal services contract.

Meanwhile, back in Indianapolis, the three players involved in that deal – Gretzky, goalie Eddie Mio and forward Peter Driscoll – were climbing into another jet. Destination: unknown.

As veteran players, Mio and Driscoll had a unique view of Gretzky in his brief career as a Racer. Without mentioning it to him, they were to be his watchdogs.

"Whitey Stapleton, the coach, had asked us to keep an eye out for him because he was a good player but a really young kid," Mio says. "We had a house near where he was boarding with a doctor and his family, and we'd go by from time to time and see how he was doing. That sort of thing."

They knew he was a teenager, that he had signed for a pretty good buck with a pretty big bonus. They knew he was a Grade 11 kid with a nice new car. So they found out the name of his favourite hang-out,

the Stake and Shake. They would cruise by there, too, especially on Friday nights, because the Racers never played on Fridays unless they were on the road. They didn't mind. They liked the kid, and he sure looked like he could play hockey, which would help put money in their pockets.

"So what happens?" Mio asks. "We get called into Whitey's office. 'You guys have been traded,' he says. 'You're going with the kid.'

"We ask him where to. He says he doesn't know. 'Just go home, pack all the stuff you can get on a plane and go to the airport by 2 p.m. There'll be a jet there to pick you up. You can get the rest of your stuff later.'

"So, okay, we go to the airport. Pretty soon Gretz comes wandering in with his stuff. He doesn't know where we're going, either. All we've heard is that it's Winnipeg or Edmonton, and there's a deadline, and whoever gets $200,000 in the bank first wins.

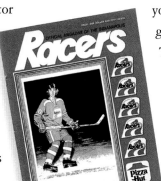

Pieces of history: tickets to Wayne's first two WHA games in Indianapolis and the first of many appearances on pro hockey's game programs.

"We load our stuff on this Learjet. It's a small one, and we've got so much stuff I almost have to sit in the aisle. We still don't know where we're going. But that's okay, because neither does the pilot.

"'Who's paying for this flight?' he asks. We tell him we don't know. He says somebody's got to. Well, Gretz was 17. He couldn't have a credit card. Peter, he pays cash for everything. So here's good old Eddie, signing for a Learjet trip on his bank VISA card. The trip figures to cost about $10,000 and the card's got a $300 limit, but what the hell ..."

They touched down in Minneapolis to go through customs.

"Where are you going?" the agent asks.

"We don't know," they reply. "Maybe Winnipeg. Maybe Edmonton." The pilot is no help. He doesn't know yet, either. They take off again. The word comes by radio: it's Edmonton. They're going to be Edmonton Oilers.

They land at Edmonton International. There's no one there to meet them. They're at the wrong airport. They take off again and land at the municipal strip where the press had gathered. The snowdrifts are higher than Mio's head. They're in the middle of the worst cold spell in years, wearing waistlength leather jackets.

It is a momentous occasion. Something historic is called for.

"Hey," says Eddie Mio. "Who's gonna cover this credit card?"

*"You guys have been traded.
You're going with the kid."*

WHITEY STAPLETON

As Gretzky's career blossomed in Edmonton, signed Oilers programs soared to No. One on the collectors' priority list. Before long, he needed outside help to sort his fan mail.

WAYNE WHO?

Eddie Mio remembers the first time he heard about Wayne Gretzky. He was in a bar in Windsor, Ontario, having a cool one after playing slo-pitch softball in a charity tournament. Years later he would be best man at the Gretzky wedding, but at that moment he was not particularly impressed.

"Think about it, now," he says. "I'm standing there, it was probably my third year in pro hockey. I've already had half a season in Indy. I've got a good name there. I'm maybe 24, and I figure I'm on my way up. I don't know anything about this Gretzky kid, or the signing, or anything.

"People keep coming up to me and saying, 'Hey, how's it gonna feel, playing with Wayne Gretzky?'

"'Wayne who?' I ask.

"They look at me like I'm from another planet.

"'Wayne Gretzky!' they say. They can't believe I haven't heard about him. Finally, I've had about enough of this stuff. I'm a third-year pro, and they're all excited about some kid? So I give it to them.

"'You better rephrase that question,' I tell them. 'How is Wayne Gretzky gonna feel playing with Eddie Mio?'"

Eight games into the season, when Gretzky, Mio and Peter Driscoll were shipped to the Edmonton Oilers, Mio was still wondering what all the fuss was about.

"Peter and I can tell our grandchildren that we were part of an historic trade," he says. "But you know how dumb we were? We thought we were the key players in the deal. You might say history kinda proved otherwise."

Above: *No fanfare, no media scrum: Larry Gordon, VP of the WHA Oilers, had the snack tray ready when Peter Driscoll, Gretzky and Eddie Mio arrived from Indianapolis in 1978.*

DESTINED TO SUCCEED

Mary Gretzky knew all along her grandson was going to be rich and famous. "Hairy arms," she'd say, in tones that brooked no argument. "In old country, we know: when you're young and have lots of hair on your back and arms, that means you're going to be rich person."

But Mary Gretzky was not one to leave such matters to the fates. If her Polish ancestry steeped her in the old beliefs, it also taught her that life is for the self-sufficient and it never hurts to help the fates along. When five-year-old Wayne confided to her that one day he was going to have a car of his own, she started putting little bits of her pension money aside. Not in the bank – in the ground.

When Wayne turned 16,

she was ready. "I'm going to buy you a car," she told him. But her grandson had inherited those self-sufficiency genes. He declined with many thanks, even after she confided that, naturally, she knew he'd pay her back.

A year later, when Wayne turned professional, he used some of his bonus money to buy a new Pontiac Trans-Am and drove it to the farm.

"Look, Grandma," he said. "How do you like my

new car?" Mary Gretzky looked at her grandson, looked at the car and thought of the money stashed away in bits and pieces for the past 11 years.

"Now what am I going to do with the $4,000?" she asked.

Mary Gretzky stayed on the farm as the years went by caring for Ellen and never letting things like illness or heart seizures keep her long from her beloved garden. She lived

to see her grandson married, flying to Edmonton in the care of a nurse in deference to her failing health. "Nice," she beamed, gazing at Wayne and Janet. "Very nice."

Granny Goalie died six months later at 88. Wayne flew in for the funeral, then flew to Pittsburgh for a game against Mario Lemieux and the Penguins. "Granny would love to have watched that one," he said. "And maybe she did."

"*Ain't it something?
One kid is 17, the other
is 23, and the line is
still the oldest in hockey
because of the old goat
on right wing!*"

GORDIE HOWE,
*51, on playing with son
Mark (right of Gretzky)
and Wayne for the 1979
WHA All-Stars. At far
right: Gretzky's future coach
in L.A., Robbie Ftorek.*

CHAPTER FOUR

THE DYNASTY

The
trophies, awards,

paintings, plaques, sticks, citations and memorabilia now spill out of the basement room on Varadi Avenue to Wayne Gretzky's restaurant in Toronto, his home in Los Angeles and the Hockey Hall of Fame. There is hardly a major hockey bauble he hasn't won, and most he's won in multiples. But the collection is short by two — the Calder Trophy as the National Hockey League's rookie of the year and the 1979-80 Art Ross Trophy as its scoring champion.

Facing page: *Gretzky and the Grail. "Before the deciding game in 1984 my dad kidded me about the Stanley Cup being awfully heavy. 'Don't you worry,' I said. 'I'll lift it if it weighs a thousand pounds.'"*
Above: *The puck that beat Vancouver's Glen Hanlon for Gretzky's first NHL goal, November 14, 1979.*

Missing those awards shot two holes through the greatest potential Grand Slam in the history of any sport, anywhere: the league's co-scoring champion, most valuable player, most gentlemanly player and rookie of the year, all wrapped up in one skinny 19-year-old with a 99 on his back.

It would have been – some say should have been – a clean sweep. There were no other individual trophies he could win. The Norris Trophy was for defencemen, the Vezina for goalkeepers. Even in light of the wonders he was to accomplish down the road, it would have been something special. It wasn't to be – partly because of the NHL's somewhat contradictory view of scoring statistics, and partly because the league wasn't going to let the World Hockey Association refugees into the lodge without one last backhand across the mouth.

Hockey's version of the Seven Years War had been costly for both leagues (one NHL estimate: a combined $100 million U.S.). With the 1979-80 season, the war was over, but the NHL was not about to forget who had started

it by daring to form in the first place. WHA franchises had gone for $25,000 each in 1972. Now the Edmonton Oilers, Winnipeg Jets, Quebec Nordiques and New England Whalers were joining the NHL, and the NHL was setting the price: $6 million apiece. Oh, and by the way, they would have to give back all the former NHL players they had signed, pay $125,000 for each of these players they reclaimed in an "expansion" draft and split the $6.35 million "close-down cost" of folding the Birmingham Bulls and Cincinnati Stingers.

Beyond the money, there were the mind games the league would play with its new partners. Psychologically it couldn't accept them as equals. That would grant retroactive equality to the league it had just beaten. So these new kids on the block had to be painted as the weak-kneed ones with glasses and sensible shoes, doomed to be

devoured by the muscle-bound behemoths of the real big league.

In Wayne's case, they were whistling past the graveyard. The Gretzky kid had found a home with the Oilers, and coach and general manager Glen Sather was assembling a set of young guns that would soon blow them out of the water.

"It's something I'll always wonder," says Eddie Mio. "What would have happened if he had gone to Winnipeg? In that first year he came to the perfect team for a young kid, a team with a lot of veterans. We had "Ace" Bailey, "Cowboy" Flett, Bill Goldsworthy, Paul Shmyr, Denis Sobchuk – people who'd been around and knew the ropes. These guys took him under their wing in that first year. Heck, everybody could see what he was going to be. It was like everybody wanted to be part of making sure he started right."

They did a heck of a job. In a league that made up for a lack of grade-A depth by playing fire-wagon, to-hell-with-defence, let's-just-outscore-'em hockey, the new kid found the perfect venue to polish his blossoming talents. He arrived from Indianapolis with three goals and three assists and finished with 46 goals, 64 assists and 110 points, good for third place in league scoring. The WHA rookie-of-the-year award was a foregone conclusion.

No. 99 was wide open to make the pass that set up the Oilers' first NHL goal in Northlands Coliseum.

"Everybody could see what he was going to be. It was like everybody wanted to be part of making sure he started right."

EDDIE MIO

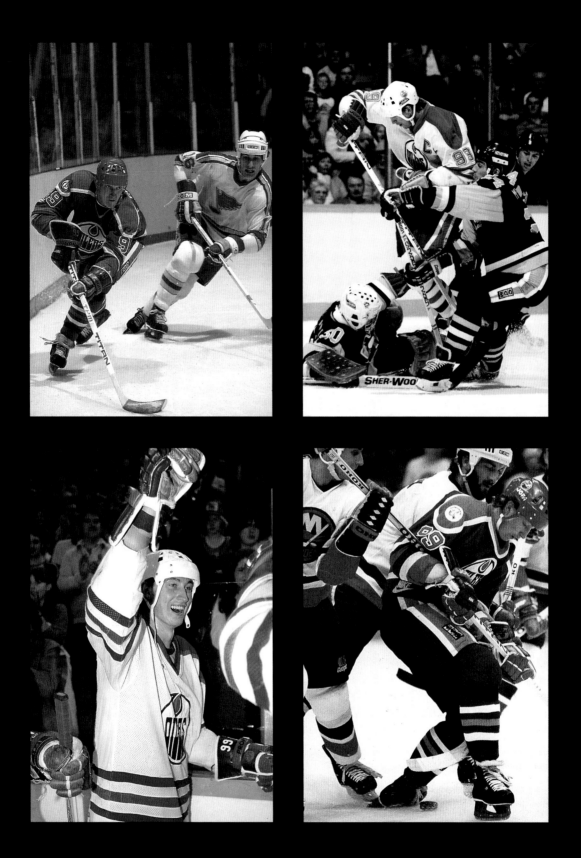

"There was this huge fuss, everybody saying Gretz this and Gretz that, and I thought, 'Why? Here's this kid, he looks about five feet nine inches and maybe 165 pounds. What's the big deal?'"

RON LOW

The NHL didn't exactly scoff. The attitude was more condescending: the Gretzky kid might have been hot stuff in the baby league, but wait till he got a taste of NHL checking. Bad scouting. Anyone who had watched him work his way through minor hockey could have explained how he reacted to suggestions that he would never do this year what he had done the year before.

Edmonton Journal sports columnist John Short was doing PR for the Oilers in that first NHL season. He can remember almost to the minute when Gretzky got the motivation to make them stick it in their ear. "We were in Maple Leaf Gardens to play the Leafs," he says. "It was early in the season, and he was reading an article in a game program. It said he'd been pretty hot stuff in the WHA, finishing third in the scoring, but there was no way in the world he'd ever finish that high in the NHL. He read it again, looked up at me and said, 'Third. I've got to finish at least third.'"

Although it didn't seem so at first, Gretzky's timing again was impeccable. In Glen Sather's first dip in the NHL draft, he had picked the oldtime scouts clean.

His first three choices? Defenceman Kevin Lowe, a semi-controlled missile named Glenn Anderson and a muscular kid named Mark Messier, who the previous year had played five games with Indianapolis and the rest with Cincinnati. The first four of his young guns were in place, and No. 99 had his launching pad. (The following year he grabbed

The Great One's NHL rookie jersey, 1979-80.

Paul Coffey, Jari Kurri and goalie Andy Moog; the year after that, another goalie named Grant Fuhr.)

Someday when there's a real world hockey league and historians marvel that the professional game was once limited to a few cities in North America, people are going to spend a lot of time analyzing the '80s Oilers and wondering what set them apart. Ron Low could tell them. He was there, watching it

happen. Even today, he shakes his head. He got his first look at Gretzky in the Oilers' first NHL season, as goaltender for the Quebec Nordiques in a game in Edmonton. "There was this huge fuss, everybody saying Gretz this and Gretz that, and I thought, 'Why? Here's this kid, he looks about five feet nine inches and maybe 165 pounds. What's the big deal?'

"So here he comes down the wing and winds up for a slap shot. I go all the way out to the faceoff circle to take away his angle. Every option he's got is cut off. There is no way he can score. And all of a sudden the puck is passed over to B.J. MacDonald and it's an empty-net goal. I swear to you, there was no pass there, and he made one."

A month later, Low was traded to the Oilers. Now he got to watch Gretzky practise every day. The games were often dazzling, but it was those practice sessions that got to Low. The championship teams, he maintains, were forged and tempered in those daily sessions. "He made every player who was with him a better player because he would do things, and they would always try to emulate him. Mark Messier wasn't really a good player in the first couple of years. His role was different. He was a tough guy, a moose. In his third year, he was unbelievable. Same with Glenn Anderson. Wayne made everybody rise up a level, and it was a constant thing, every day."

*"People look at the NHL and they see a game. Well, sure it's
a game, but it's also our job. And it's like any other job. If you're not ready
to work every day, you'll lose it. And who'd want to lose a job like this?"*

WAYNE GRETZKY

*In hockey as life, triumph rests heavily on preparation. Stretches, wind-sprints,
medical checks on the stationary bike, trucking from one rink to another
rather than miss a practice — all were ingredients in the Oilers dynasty.*

Gretzky was the centrepiece, the focal point, the one weapon no one else could match. But the Oilers were not just Gretzky. The team was an extraordinary collection of young and burgeoning talent in just the right place with just the right coach: Sather. The veterans from that team, today scattered all over the NHL, understand better now than then just what the man called "Slats" brought to the mix, on and off the ice.

"We were all so young, just basically a bunch of hayseeds," says Kevin Lowe. "And here was Slats, a fairly cosmopolitan guy. He encouraged the dressing up thing, the good restaurants thing. He taught us that it wasn't just a business, it was also a game to be enjoyed. The first time we were in the finals, against the Islanders, he said, 'Listen, this is the Stanley Cup final. Some of you may never get this far again. Relax and enjoy the experience.'"

The rapier and the broadsword: Gretzky and Mark Messier.

"He doesn't get nearly enough credit for what we became," Messier agrees. "I don't buy the business of us being cocky. Hell, we were so naive I doubt we knew what cocky meant. The thing was, Glen allowed us to grow up without taking away any of the creativity on the ice. People talk about chemistry. Well, chemistry is good-quality people with talent working towards the same goals. Glen gathered the talent and let us play our way."

While the dancers were dancing, Sather made sure the foot soldiers were there to slog. He had superb goaltending and fronted it with tough, stay-at-home defencemen to go with the blazing offensive thrust of Coffey. And to protect the dancers, he had Sammy: Dave Semenko, the tough and truculent winger who patrolled Gretzky's left side like a hit man waiting for his next contract. In later years he would pass the brass knuckles on to

Marty McSorley, but it was Sammy who set the ground rules for teams that dared trifle with the stars.

One of Sather's many strengths was the ability to pull in a role player, a journeyman on another team who would, in his own way, become a key ingredient in the mix. Such a man was McSorley, who came to the Oilers in 1985 after two indifferent seasons with the Pittsburgh Penguins. Right away, he knew that he was going to be a part of something special.

"There was that quiet confidence – all right, arrogance – that came with the two Stanley Cups they already had. I stepped into a scenario where they'd had three or four years together and won a lot. They looked at players coming in to fill the holes and they accepted them. Wayne always let everyone know how important they were to the organization, right to the 20th guy. When I walked into the dressing room for the first time, he came over and congratulated me on coming to the team. It was like I was family.

"It was an incredible feeling, to know you were surrounded by the best people in the game, from Sather and John Muckler and Ted Green, and all that on-ice talent. Then, after they lost the '86 division final to Calgary, they came back and added Kent Nilsson ("The most talented hockey player I've ever seen," says Gretzky) and Reijo Ruotsalainen. You could see Sather working, replacing some pieces, adding others."

> *"Well, chemistry is good-quality people with talent working towards the same goals. Glen gathered the talent and let us play our way."*
>
> **MARK MESSIER**

"I always thought the NHL should pay part of his salary. He was filling their rinks wherever he went."

MAX MCNAB

Executive vice-president, New Jersey Devils.

McSorley looks at the '87 team and sees the best team ever. "You had the best players in the world in given situations. The best power forward in Mark Messier, the best skating defenceman in Paul Coffey, the best goalie in Grant Fuhr, the best centre in Wayne, the best shooter in Jari Kurri, one of the fastest forwards in Glenn Anderson, a second goalie in Andy Moog who could have been a star anywhere else, and all that run by arguably the best coach in the game."

McSorley underplays his own role in the circus, but he and Semenko were as key in their own way as the unflappable Fuhr in goal. Policemen, muscle, menace, whatever the term, by their very presence they gave Gretzky and friends the freedom to roll. "The way we played, there were nights we gave up a lot of goals," Gretzky says. "But we knew that we could score a bunch, and that when it got right down to it, Grant would slam the door."

How good were the Oilers? Lowe had to go away to find out. "I didn't really have a good appreciation for what we'd done until I came to the Rangers and started playing with guys who'd played against us for a

lot of years. The things they tell me now about us – hey, I took all those things for granted. Four-hundred-goal seasons and Stanley Cups were what I expected. Now people give us our place in history, and I guess we were pretty special. But the key was Gretz. To build a team like that, you've got to start with a superstar. Not to downgrade the rest, but he made it happen."

Not that the Oilers tore the league apart right away. They spent much of the first half of their first NHL season in or near last place. They didn't make the last playoff spot until the final week. But Gretzky was flying.

At mid-season he stood third behind Marcel Dionne of the Kings and Montreal's Guy Lafleur, but trailed Dionne by 26. He caught him in Game 77 with two goals and four assists in an 8-5 win over the Leafs in Maple Leaf Gardens. "He missed a backhand in the last few seconds with the goalie down," Walter Gretzky recalls. "Put the darn thing over the net, over the

Sports Illustrated's *Grecian Amphora, awarded to Wayne Gretzky, 1982 Sportsman of the Year.*

glass, over everything. We laughed about it, but later he said, 'Wouldn't it be funny, Wally, if I lost the scoring title by one point?'"

He did, and it wasn't funny at all.

On the last day he was on top, two points ahead of Dionne, who had one game left. He'd lost 11 pounds and one game to the tonsillitis that had dragged him down since mid-October. But if the Vancouver Canucks could hold Dionne to a point, the title was his.

Dionne got two assists. They finished tied at 137 points. Gretzky was disappointed, but figured, what the heck, at least they would share the trophy. They didn't. Under NHL rules, in a tie the Art Ross Trophy went to the player who had scored the greatest number of goals. Dionne had 53, Gretzky, 51.

"I'm just polishing it for Wayne," Dionne said. "He's going to have it lots of times."

Sure. But not that time. And you never get a second shot at being a rookie. For that matter, Wayne never got a first one. Heading into the first merger season, the NHL announced that statistics compiled by WHA players would not count in their NHL career totals. The official excuse was that the WHA teams had played overtime games and the NHL did not. Actually, it was that last slap in the mouth – the implication that the WHA was a minor league like the American and the Central. Having demoted the WHA, the NHL ruled that

"But the key was Gretz. To build a team like that, you've got to start with a superstar. Not to downgrade the rest, but he made it happen."

KEVIN LOWE

January 7, 1984: Gretzky pots his 25th NHL hat trick with goals No. 48, 49 and 50 of the season, against the Hartford Whalers in Edmonton.

first-year NHLers who had played in the WHA weren't eligible for the Calder Trophy rookie-of-the-year competition. Why? Because, quote, "They have played a full season with a major professional league." The WHA wasn't major enough to have its players' statistics count in NHL totals, but it was somehow major enough to keep its players from being considered NHL rookies.

Still, the last laugh was Gretzky's. The league that wouldn't let him be rookie of the year and wouldn't give him a share of the Art Ross Trophy had to present him with his first Hart Trophy as most valuable player. Everyone knew it wasn't going to be the last. "One down, Wally," Gretzky whispered as he rose from the table to head for the stage. "One down, and counting."

The years have put such a glorious and deserved lustre on the Oilers of the '80s it is easy to forget that the road to the top was twisted, treacherous and laced with speed bumps.

Double play, 1980: the Lady Byng Trophy as the league's most-gentlemanly player and the Hart Trophy as its most-valuable.

"We were kids," Gretzky says. "And we acted like kids. We wanted the Stanley Cup, but we had no idea of the kind of commitment it took to win it." It was a learning process. Even as he piled up the personal points at an unheard-of rate, the lessons and the price paid for them put him and his teammates on an emotional teeter-totter.

- 1979-80: The Oilers sneaked into the last playoff spot and got swept in three tough games by the Philadelphia Flyers.

- 1980-81: The kids were a year older, maybe more than a year better. They finished fourth in their division, 14th overall, and stunned the NHL by sweeping the mighty Montreal Canadiens in three games to open the playoffs in one of the greatest upsets in Stanley Cup history. Then they ran smack into the defending-champion New York Islanders, who bottled Gretzky and took them out in six games.

From a personal standpoint the regular season was a triumph. Gretzky broke Bobby Orr's single-season assist record of 102 with 109, and Phil Esposito's total-point mark of 152 with 164. But Walter

Gretzky was starting to hear and read the words that drove him nuts: "He'll never be the greatest until he has a Stanley Cup ring."

- 1981-82: The season beyond belief: 50 goals in 39 games, a staggering 92 in 80, plus 120 assists and an unheard-of 212 points to sweep the record book clean. "Who knows where he'll stop?" asked assistant coach John Muckler. "Is 300 points impossible? Probably. But if anybody could ever do it, this would be the one."

The Oilers had finished second to the Islanders and scored an outrageous 417 goals (a record they would lift to 424, then 446 in the next two seasons). Cocky, obnoxious, full of themselves as only the young can be, they followed it with one of the biggest collapses in playoff history.

The Los Angeles Kings, who had finished 47 points behind them in the standings, knocked them out, three games to two, in the first round. They blew a 4-1 lead in one game, but the crusher was Game Three, the one that came to be known as the Miracle on Manchester, for the street that fronted the Fabulous Forum. In that one the Oilers led 5-0 and lost 6-5 in overtime. "Weak-Kneed Wimps!" screamed *The Edmonton Sun* when it was over. The summer grew even longer.

- 1982-83: His ice time cut from 26 minutes a game to 22, Gretzky "cooled" to a mere 71 goals, but boosted his assist record to 125 and with 196 points, won the scoring title by 72 points over Quebec's Peter Stastny and picked up his fourth straight Hart Trophy.

A LESSON LEARNED

Championship teams have an extra ingredient that doesn't show on any scouting report and cannot be measured by any known test. The 1983 Edmonton Oilers discovered that four games too late in the Stanley Cup final.

They had every reason to believe they had a shot against the defending-champion New York Islanders. Gretzky was coming off a record 195-point season carrying his fourth straight Hart Trophy. Mark Messier had his first 50-goal season. Jari Kurri was flying. Grant Fuhr, the best goalkeeper in the business, was guarding their nets. Okay, the Islanders had a great team, but this one was great, too.

The Oilers went out in four straight. Gretzky's total point contribution: four assists. The Islanders pounded them.

When they pressed the New York net, there was the truculent Billy Smith, brandishing his goalie stick like an axe and more than occasionally using it as such. It wasn't a battle, it was a rout.

An hour after the fourth game ended, Gretzky and Kevin Lowe walked past the open door of the Islanders' dressing room. It looked like an emergency ward. Bryan Trottier was icing a bad knee. Denis Potvin was having a shoulder treated. The Islanders were a mass of bloody lips, black eyes and body bruises.

The lesson sunk in. "They took more punishment than we did," Gretzky says. "They dove into more boards, stuck their faces in front of more pucks, threw their bodies into more pileups. They sacrificed everything they had. 'That's what wins championships,' Kevin said. We learned it the hard way."

And this time, the Oilers got it almost right, crushing Winnipeg, Calgary and Chicago to reach the Cup final before falling in four straight to the Islanders. Gretzky's series contribution: no goals, four assists. All together, now: "He'll never be the greatest until he wears that ring."

■ 1983-84: Bingo. Grown-up time. It began with a gesture by long-time Oilers captain Lee Fogolin just before the season started. "Here," he told Gretzky, "I want you to have the C." It was not lightly given, nor lightly accepted. Fogolin was telling the kids it was their team now, their responsibility. Determined to be equal to it, they roared back to the final against the Islanders, who were gunning for their fifth straight championship.

For Gretzky, the awards continued to pour in. Another scoring title, another Hart Trophy, another car at the all-star game, a record-shattering 51 straight games from the season opener with at least a point (and a staggering three-a-game average with 61 goals and 92 assists). None of these things would mean anything if he didn't get to lift that Cup.

They took the Islanders in five games, winning the last one at home. The next morning, Gretzky, Messier, Coffey and Lowe met at his apartment. "We're taking Stanley

for a walk," Gretzky said, and away they went, touring restaurants and bars and putting the Cup up where Edmontonians could touch it and have their picture taken with it. "These people have waited a long time," he said. "It's their Cup, too."

It was to be theirs for three years out of the next four; the Oilers' own drive-for-five stopped in mid-stride in 1985-86 when they lost the Smythe Division final to Calgary in seven games. There were three more scoring titles for Gretzky before Mario Lemieux relegated him to second in 1987-88, by which time Gretzky already knew the heady Edmonton days were over.

While still young in age, they were old in experience. In business terms they were well-used assets (with a potentially huge payroll) who could be sold off while market value was still high. "I came back for that '87-'88 season and Coff wasn't there," McSorley recalls. "It started out as a money problem and then got personal between him and Sather. He'd been traded to Pittsburgh. Moog had gone to the Canadian national team. He'd

have stayed, but he wanted to be recognized as a top-notch goaltender, and with Fuhr there he wasn't going to get the chance. They let Nilsson and Ruotsalainen go back to Europe. You could see the signs. They'd sort of stepped sideways from a team that could totally dominate finesse-wise to a defence of Steve Smith, Kevin Lowe, Charlie Huddy, Craig Muni, Randy Gregg and myself. It wasn't an offensive defence the way it had been. They were willing to give up a bit because they thought they could still win."

McSorley doesn't buy that the team's fear of growing old together was the reason for change. More likely it was sheer economics. Whatever it was, rumours were flying that there were no untouchables, that more changes would follow and that one of those moved might be Gretzky himself.

The Oilers didn't believe it. Not Gretzky. Pocklington wouldn't dare. Gretzky wasn't that sure. "The night we won the Cup, we were having a steam," says Kurri. "Wayne told me then he might not be coming back. I looked at him like he'd gone crazy."

Ten years after the 17-year-old had climbed aboard the plane in Indianapolis not knowing where he would land, Gretzky had come full circle: he knew he was going. He just didn't know where.

Denied a share of the Art Ross Trophy when he tied Marcel Dionne for the league scoring title as a rookie, Gretzky won it for the next seven years, and 10 to date.

"Wayne told me then he might not be coming back. I looked at him like he'd gone crazy."

JARI KURRI

*Gretzky and the 1988 Cup:
the final celebratory tour of the
rink after 10 years as an Oiler.*

BROKEN RECORDS

By 1981-82 the 50-goal season had been reached 54 times. For some, like Phil Esposito, Bobby Hull and Guy Lafleur, it had become almost routine. But one record seemed unassailable.

Maurice "The Rocket" Richard had potted 50 goals in 50 games for the 1944-45 Montreal Canadiens. That one, they said, might last forever. Sure, a guy could get more than 50 – but could he get 50 in the first 50 games?

Gretzky provided the answer before the year – not the season – was out. On December 30, 1981, playing at home against Philadelphia, he scored five times in a 7-5 victory, putting No. 50 into an empty net in the closing seconds of the 39th game.

"We weren't ready for it," says Bill Tuele, Oilers media director, who was planning the celebration. "How do you plan for a five-goal night?"

But 50-in-39 was merely the appetizer. For the single-season record for goals, assists and points, the legend Wayne chased was himself. He finished the 1981-82 season with 92 goals, 120 assists and 212 points, an NHL record.

The man whose record he was destroying at that point was a legend in his own right – the Italian Slot Machine, Phil Esposito,

whose single-season mark of 76 goals and 152 points, set as a Boston Bruin, had stood since 1970-71.

Esposito followed the Oilers as Gretzky drew closer to breaking the records so that he could be there to offer his congratulations, as Gretzky himself will try to be there if and when his own marks fall.

"The game is changing," Gretzky said. "Players are so much bigger and faster now. Kids are taking power-skating. Who knows where the top is, or how many goals or assists or points

someone will get in a season? That's why records are there – to be broken by someone else."

Four years later Gretzky upped the assist mark to 163 and the point total to 215. Now when people spoke of Gretzky, it was in terms of one man – Gordie Howe, who had played longer, scored more goals and collected more points than anyone.

Above: *Gretzky becomes the filling for an Oiler sandwich after scoring his record-setting 77th goal.*

Above: *December 30, 1981. The first of the Gretzky Impossibles: 50 goals in 39 games to tie the record first set by Maurice Richard in 50 games.*
Below: *February 24, 1982. The next Impossible: Gretzky beats Buffalo's Don Edwards to break Phil Esposito's single-season scoring record of 76 goals.*

THE STREAK

On the night of January 22, 1984, a friend of Walter Gretzky's sat in Vancouver watching via satellite dish as the Oilers played a home game against the L.A. Kings. In Brantford, Walter had his own dish going. They had spoken earlier about how important the game was because of the – well, that thing they were too superstitious to discuss.

It was the Oilers' 52nd game of the season. Wayne had at least one point in each of the first 51. The only comparable record in sport was Joe Dimaggio's 56-game hitting streak with the old New York Yankees. In Las Vegas bookies were giving 500-1 that he couldn't stretch The Streak (by then it was in capitals) through all 80 games.

Gretzky's shoulder was hurt. The Streak was wobbling. In Game 44 against the Chicago Black Hawks, he'd kept it alive by blocking a clearing pass, knocking the puck down with his hand and putting it into the empty net with one second left.

The Streak was alive heading into the L.A. game, even though Kings goalie Markus Mattsson was trying to kill it. Mattsson was stoning Gretzky.

In the second period, he and defenceman Charlie Huddy broke in on Matts-son. Gretzky deked, drew the goalie over and fed a soft little pass to Huddy, who was staring at an empty net. The assist was a cinch. The Streak was alive. Charlie shot, and missed by a mile.

The man in Vancouver began a countdown: "Five … four … three …"

On two, the phone rang. He picked it up. "Hello, Wally," he said.

"Did you see that?" whispered Walter Gretzky. "Did you see that?"

The Streak died that night. Wayne was just as happy to see it go. Charlie got over his disappointment. And eventually, Walter got back to liking him.

But it took a while.

Above: *"The longer it ran, the more pressure I felt. I was almost relieved when it ended."* Wayne Gretzky on his season-opening 51-game point streak.

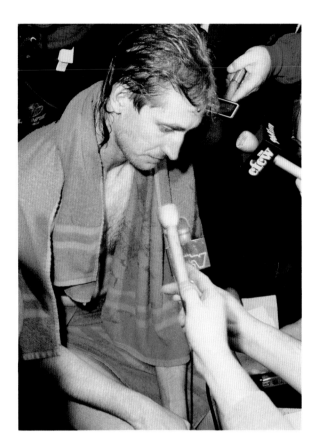

THE MEDIA GAME

More than once early in his career, Gretzky came to the conclusion that playing the game was the easy part. The problems came in the never-ending game called Jock Meets Media.

Now he has dealt with the cameras, microphones, notepads and the people behind them for so long he could do it in his sleep. Sometimes, slumped in front of his locker or trying to get an arm into a shirt with 50 reporters jammed close enough to examine his pores, he probably does. There isn't a hockey question he hasn't answered hundreds of times. The media are as tired of asking as he is of answering, but both sides know it is a

game that must be played.

"The biggest press conference we ever had, by far, was Wayne's first NHL appearance in Toronto," says Oilers media director Bill Tuele. "As a rule we'd just hold a press conference at the rink after practice. For this one we had to rent a hotel ballroom. The final head count was 135.

"Wayne was kind of taken aback. He hadn't expected anything like this. So what's the first question?

"'Gretzky! That's Polish,

isn't it? How do you feel about the situation with Solidarity in Poland?'

"'I'm just a hockey player,' Wayne told him. 'I don't know enough about politics in Poland to discuss them.' That's when I knew he'd be okay."

That Toronto visit was also memorable because Luciano Pavarotti was in town for a concert. The word was that the toughest quinella was tickets to both Pavarotti and Gretzky – and that Gretzky was the harder of the two.

How hard? Wayne needed tickets for Phyllis and Walter. There were none to be had. Finally he autographed a hockey stick and gave it to Brent.

"Take this outside," he told him. "Find a scalper. Get two good seats."

Brent dashed out onto Carleton Street, waving the stick. It was good for two in the reds. The Gretzkys saw their son's Toronto NHL debut.

"Next time," Wally told him, "bring extra sticks."

NEVER MESS WITH MICKEY

For the first five years of his pro career the media complained that Wayne Gretzky was too quiet, never offered an opinion on anything. In 1984 he let loose with one teensy opinion, and suddenly he was a smart mouth.

The two words that did him in? Mickey Mouse.

It happened after a game in Edmonton in which the Oilers had pounded the New Jersey Devils 13-4. The Devils goalie for the first two periods was Wayne's old teammate and friend Ron Low. Wayne was so embarrassed for him and for "Chico" Resch, the third-period victim, that he cut loose at the Devils organization in the post-game media scrum. "They're putting a Mickey-Mouse operation on the ice," he said. "They'd better start getting some better personnel. It's ruining hockey."

In New Jersey, sales of Mickey Mouse ears skyrocketed. The fans couldn't wait for the rematch on their home ice. When Wayne looked up at the crowd, all he could see was a forest of ears. Fans who had been staying away in droves now had a reason to see at least one game a year. They had the guy who'd called their team Mickey Mouse.

The irony was that Gretzky had spoken more out of concern for his friend, and Ron Low was never all that bothered about it. "I'd just been traded to New Jersey, and it was one bad team. In the first two periods, they put six by me, and the coach, Billy MacMillan, says, 'I'm gonna get you outa there in the third.'

"'Don't do it,' I said. 'I think they're trying to stop. You throw Chico in there, it'll be like fresh meat.' And it was true. Near the end of the second period they only took a couple of shots. They'd called off the dogs. Gretz used to do that a lot. I swear there were nights when he could have got 15 points. But they didn't want to embarrass anyone.

"'Don't do it,' I said again. But he did, and they pumped seven past Chico in the third."

Above: Loyal Devils fans were all ears on Gretzky's next visit to New Jersey.

OH, CANADA!

Gretzky's first taste of international hockey came in the 1977 Junior World Cup competition in Montreal. He was 16 and hearing the same old scouting report. "He's a great young player," said Ernie "Punch" McLean, one of the Team Canada coaches. "But does he have the strength to take it in the rough going?"

They named him to the team anyway, more or less on spec. Canada lost 3-2 to the Russians, but he made the first all-star team and won the scoring title with eight goals and nine assists in six games.

Gretzky played in four Canada Cup series – 1981, 1984, 1987 and 1991 – and was the leading scorer in all of them as Canada won the last three after a humiliating 8-1 loss to the Russians in the '81 final.

Igor Larionov remembers that game vividly. Canada had beaten the Russians twice in preliminary games. "In Russia we play man on man and I am centre, so Gretzky is my check. But he is behind the net, and we do not play that game.

"The day of the final I went with associate coach and we stood by the goal-judge cage looking out at the place behind the net. We spend two hours discussing what I must do

there, how I must play him. I don't know, I guess he had an off night, because we win 8-1. But back there, it is a different game the way he plays it."

Canada Cup 1987 saw Gretzky and Mario Lemieux as teammates and linemates – a match made in heaven. Wayne set up all of Mario's four goals in the best-of-three final against the Russians. Two of them are legend – one in the second overtime of Game Two to tie the

series; and the series winner with 1:26 remaining in the third period of Game Three.

Gretzky dropped the puck back to Lemieux, who snapped a howitzer into the net. Gretzky leapt into his arms and dragged him to the ice in a bear hug. That one made every hockey highlight video.

Above: *Gretzky in familiar form during the 1981 Canada Cup.*

"Mario had those awesome wrists, and he could get the puck away so quickly. He's six-foot-four with the touch on the puck of a guy five-foot-six, and he could put one through a refrigerator door. I may not be a genius, but I knew who should be passing and who should be shooting. I told him, 'If we get two-on-ones, get me the puck. I pass, you shoot.'"

WAYNE GRETZKY

GENERAL WALLY

For Wayne, Walter Gretzky was more than a father; he was a confidant, long-distance coach and a strategist. He was also a heck of an amateur psychologist.

In 1984, Wally was in Brantford watching the Stanley Cup quarter-final against the Calgary Flames on TV, a confrontation that was throwing more fuel on "The Battle of Alberta." Young in seasons, the Calgary-Edmonton hockey feud was already bidding to rival that between the Montreal Canadiens and Toronto Maple Leafs. The Oilers had led the series 3-1, but now it was 3-2. Wayne was not playing well. "No jump," Wally said. "No strength. When he tries to turn, he falls down."

Wally and Phyllis got on a plane. "He plays better when his mother's there," Wally explained. The Flames won Game Six in Calgary. Wayne had the flu, but why was he falling so much?

"What skates are you wearing?" Wally asked.

"The new ones," Wayne said. "The old ones are all battered up."

"Go back to the old ones. You've lost weight with the flu. Your foot is slipping in the boot. It's affecting your balance. And – you've been losing the puck off the heel of your stick. That means the stick is a bit too long. Cut it back a little."

Wayne loaded up on antibiotics, put on the old skates, trimmed the stick and scored one goal and set up two others as the Oilers won 7-4.

Did the stick and skates make any difference?

"Dunno," Wally shrugged. "But hockey players are superstitious. He was comfortable in the old skates. He'd played well in them. If he thought the short stick was better, maybe it would be."

THE HOLY GRAIL

The Oilers went to training camp for the 1983-84 season with the taste of defeat on their tongues and the lesson of the New York Islanders etched on the inner side of their eyelids. It wasn't a hockey season, it was a crusade. They had to prove to the customers and to themselves that they were the best team in hockey.

Lest they be too intense, too determined, and flame out before the playoffs, Glen Sather dangled a carrot – literally. The Stanley Cup was a carrot, he told them. It's out there for the taking. Why not grab a bite?

The Oilers bit with a vengeance. They won that Stanley Cup, and the next one. In 1985-86 they hit a speed bump, losing to the hated Flames in the Smythe division final – remembered as the one in which the Oilers defenceman Steve Smith tried to

pass from behind his own end and bounced the puck off Grant Fuhr's heel into his own net for the goal that turned the series. But they rebounded for two more championships in 1986-87 and 1987-88.

And there was always the carrot. It was there on the side of the first Stanley Cup rings, with one bite in it. After each title, the rings showed the carrot with one more bite.

You could get arguments that the Oilers of that span were the greatest team ever

assembled, or at least close to the fabled Montreal Canadiens, who won five straight Stanley Cups from 1956 through 1960. It must have seemed as though nothing could stop the Gretzky gang from making it five in six years. But Gretzky had a hunch. As the Oilers skated around Northlands Coliseum waving the Cup, Gretzky summoned them to centre ice, where they collapsed in a joyous heap for a team picture. Paul Coffey had been

shipped to Pittsburgh a year earlier. There were rumblings that more trades were coming, perhaps even the unthinkable: the trading of Gretzky himself.

Above: *In 1983, the Islanders taught the Oilers what it took to win the Stanley Cup. In 1984, the Oilers showed how well they'd learned, taking the cup in five games.* Facing page: *Parade of champions. Edmonton fans fill the streets in 1984 as Gretzky and the Oilers parade their first Stanley Cup.*

Wayne's '84, '85, '87 and '88 Stanley Cup championship rings.

"You hear, well the game has changed. It's more wide-open since expansion. Then why hasn't anyone else done what Wayne Gretzky has done? I'll tell you why. Because he's that much better than the rest of us."

BOBBY CLARKE
Philadelphia Flyers

Facing page: *Gretzky dominates the Flyers in 1985 as the Oilers win their second Stanley Cup.* Above: *The celebration in 1987 was all that much sweeter after a tough seven-game series again against the Flyers.*

Above: *Almost behind the red line, Gretzky hoists the puck over Glen Wesley's foot and skins it past the goal post in the 1988 Stanley Cup finals.*
Below: *Gretzky takes his magic show on the road to Boston.*

On May 26, 1988, the Oilers won their fourth cup in five years. They hadn't begun to reach their prime. Their average age was 25. There was every reason to believe the dynasty would roll on, that they would build a record the rest of the NHL would never touch. But the Oilers as they were that night were soon to be a memory.

"The Cup is a symbol of the championship, and once you can actually hold the championship you want to touch it, feel it, use it, show it around. You want to relish the fact that it's real, it's in your hands, that you really are the best in the world ..."

WAYNE GRETZKY

Above: *Janet Jones raises the 1988 Stanley Cup as her fiancé again sips victory.* Below: *End of an era: Bill Ranford, Esa Tikkanen, Mark Messier, Gretzky and Kevin Lowe, 1988.*

ROYAL WEDDING

Janet Jones met Wayne Gretzky for the first time in 1981, when he was a judge and she was a contestant on a show called *Dance Fever*.

Over the years they kept running into each other. Sparks did not fly. But in 1987, they met again at a Boston Celtic's game. CLICK!

All they wanted to do was get married. Given their two careers, they knew it would have to be a big wedding. What they didn't plan on was the pre-wedding circus. Canada's superstar was marrying a gorgeous American actress. Just like that, the country had its own version of a royal wedding.

Newspapers, particularly in Edmonton where the knot would be tied, scrambled for wedding stories. Fact was an early casualty. Janet's dress was said to cost $40,000, the ring $100,000. Champagne would flow like water – at $300 per bottle. None of it was true – but what a story! People known to be on the invitation list were polled to find out what they planned to give the happy couple. Janet's honeymoon lingerie was a subject for journalistic speculation.

"Let's elope," they said. But they couldn't. So they crossed their fingers and hoped – and the wedding on July 16, 1988, in St. Joseph's Cathedral-Basilica, went off like a dream.

As for the wedding presents, Alan Thicke won the unofficial award for originality. He had been present the first time Wayne and Janet had dinner together, at a Los Angeles restaurant called La Serre. He bought the cushions on the two seats they had used and had

them inscribed with their names and the date.

So, off they went on their honeymoon, prepared to return to Edmonton, buy a home, and settle in. They were still honeymooning in Los Angeles when Gretzky took the telephone call that would change their plans and the course of history in the NHL. It was Bruce McNall, owner of the L.A. Kings.

"Wayne," he said, "I've been given permission to talk to you. So, you wanna have lunch tomorrow?"

"*And in that moment when the couple — both blond and both 27 — stood on the basilica steps before plunging into the first chapter of their life together, they performed the traditional royal function of embodying the fears and joys of every citizen.*"

MACLEAN'S MAGAZINE

CHAPTER FIVE

THE KING

Wayne
Gretzky might easily

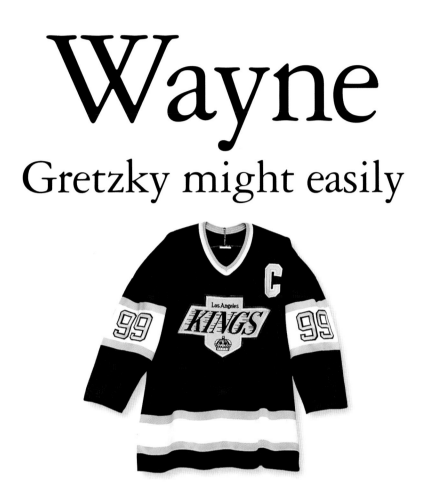

have been a Vancouver Canuck instead of a Los Angeles King. For a while, there was even a chance that he'd be a Winnipeg Jet. The deal was there for the Canucks if they wanted it in the summer of 1988. They turned it down. Then it was there for the Jets, who said yes, only to have it pulled away from them.

Facing page: *The stage was set, the theatre standing-room only. Now it was up to the leading man to make hockey a hit in Hollywood.* Above: *From the Hall of Fame collection: the jersey Gretzky wore breaking Gordie Howe's NHL record of 1,850 points.*

"I promised Mess I wouldn't do this." Gretzky wipes away the tears at the press conference confirming the Trade of the Century.

And finally, it was there for Bruce McNall, the rotund dealer in ancient coins, motion pictures and racehorses, who gulped once or twice and said go.

"I was always confident that it was the right thing to do, always confident that it would work," he says now. "I just didn't know at what level. Wayne wasn't sure, either. We'd sit around doing scenarios: 'Well, we've got 10,000 a night. What if we got 12,000 … or 13,000 … or 14,000?' I'm not sure we even considered a scenario where we'd be selling out every night. We weren't at all certain how it would play out.

"Sure, it was scary. When you're looking at $15 million for the deal, then the added expense of paying Wayne, the players surrounding him, the insurance. A to Z, it's a big obligation. And on top of that I didn't have the revenue streams from the [Great Western] Forum that would normally be able to accommodate that.

"What's happened since Wayne got here is 90 percent Wayne. But sure, there is some personal satisfaction. If we hadn't made the deal, would there have been expansion into Anaheim and San Jose and Florida? I don't think so.

We had the right player coming to the right place at the right time, and it lifted the game to a whole new level. We proved that you can sell a game without having it indigenous to the area."

But first, he had to put the deal together. And there was competition. Nelson Skalbania was attempting to get back into the hockey game. His plan: buy 25 percent of the Canucks, give Walter Gretzky some of the shares (they couldn't have gone to Wayne; the NHL would frown upon a playing owner), buy Wayne from Pocklington and move him to Vancouver.

"I knew Peter very well," says Skalbania. "I knew that he might be short of money at the time, and if he could get $15 to $20 million for Wayne now – which wouldn't be there four years down the road – and still keep the team, maybe he'd be ready to capitalize his asset.

"I had the deal with Peter. He didn't care where Wayne went. I'd chatted with Wayne, knew he liked Vancouver. I had corporate sponsors lined up. But it was conditional on my getting the 25 percent of the Canucks. They weren't interested."

Actually, they were. But not at those prices, says Arthur Griffiths, team vice-chairman and governor. "The first thing I did after Nelson's approach was talk to Peter. He outlined a deal for $15 million (U.S.), some players and futures. Basically it would have stripped the team to the bones. Then, later in the summer, he told me the deal

"I phoned Wayne and said Peter had given me permission to approach him. The minute Wayne heard that, he was finished as an Oiler."

BRUCE MCNALL

had gone up to $20 million, which he could get from Bruce McNall." Determined not to be a pawn in a bidding war, Griffiths phoned McNall and told him that if he did decide to compete it wouldn't be at anything higher than $15 million.

Rebuffed in Vancouver, Skalbania went to Winnipeg and put together a deal under which Walter would get one-quarter of the Jets for $1. The Jets agreed. But first, Skalbania had to land Gretzky. By that time, McNall was into the heavy wheeling and dealing.

"I think I had the first real discussion with Peter about Wayne at the June NHL meetings in 1987," he says. "I'd mention it again at various meetings over the year, but nothing much substantive until the playoffs of '88 when he phoned me and said, 'If you're serious, let's talk.'"

McNall was serious, all right, but things kept getting in the way – like Wayne's wedding to Janet Jones in July 1988. Six days into the honeymoon, "I phoned Wayne and said Peter had given me permission to approach him. The minute Wayne heard that, he was finished as an Oiler."

He had heard the rumours. He knew Skalbania was trying to put the Vancouver deal together. He knew Pocklington was upset because he wouldn't sign a new contract that would take him out of the personal-services class and make him part of the Oiler operation, which Peter wanted to take public as a stock issue. But the actual word that the Oilers would consider dealing him away stung Gretzky as nothing had before. "Right then," says McNall, "he became part of the trade process, discussing the players he'd like with him, how much he wanted Marty McSorley to be part of it, that sort of thing."

Talks heated up. The deal was on, then off, then on and off again. Pocklington backed off twice, once when the media got word of the negotiations and once just before the press conference in Edmonton to announce the trade. But it was done, and the hockey world rocked.

One trade – two viewpoints.

"99 TEARS!" screamed the headline on the front page of *The Edmonton Sun.* The only other item on the page was a box listing stories on the deal on 21 different pages. "Gretzky Gone" moaned *The Edmonton Journal.* Former Oilers like Eddie Mio and Paul Coffey ripped Pocklington for letting it happen. "He treated Wayne like a piece of meat," Coffey stormed. Pocklington lashed back the following day, accusing Gretzky of having "an ego the size of Manhattan" (he later apologized to Gretzky, saying the remark was taken out of context) and suggesting that the tears he'd shed at the press conference were an act. "He's a great actor," he said. "… I thought he pulled it off beautifully."

Across Canada, columnists and editorialists battled to outdo one another in expressing their outrage and grief. No one groped further than Nelson Riis, House Leader for the New Democratic Party, on the floor of Parliament. "Wayne Gretzky is a national symbol, like the beaver," he thundered. "How can we allow the sale of our national symbols? The Edmonton Oilers without Wayne Gretzky is like … *Wheel of Fortune* without Vanna White."

Janet Jones Gretzky did not escape the heat. Who was this American actress to come up here and steal Canada's greatest sports hero? She was Jezebel Janet. She even made the supermarket tabloids. "How Gretzky's pregnant Yankee bride stole him away from Canada," blared *The Star* across the top of its front page. The full-page inside spread offered "Inside story of how pregnant American wife lured Canada's hockey hero with promise of show biz fame."

> *"How can we allow the sale of our national symbols?*
> *The Edmonton Oilers without Wayne Gretzky is like …*
> Wheel of Fortune *without Vanna White."*
>
> **NELSON RIIS**

*"I remember walking on the ice, watching the Oilers warm up
and getting this weird feeling that I was standing
in the wrong end of the rink."*

WAYNE GRETZKY

*October 20, 1988. Gretzky's first game as a King in Edmonton's Northlands
Coliseum cut the final ties with the team he'd led for a decade.*

"We had the right player coming to the right place at the right time, and it lifted the game to a whole new level."

BRUCE MCNALL

Meanwhile, in Los Angeles, the trade was drawing mixed reviews. There was excitement, sure. The press conference was jammed. Movie stars and sports heroes fell over themselves saying how great it was going to be having Gretzky as a King. But they were talking about Gretzky the celebrity. In California, the sport was somewhere over the horizon behind skateboarding and beach volleyball. On most nights the Fabulous Forum was closer to empty than full. "There are 800,000 Canadians living in the L.A. area," said Jack Kent Cooke a few years after establishing the franchise in 1967. "I've just discovered why they left Canada. They hate hockey."

Now the Kings had given away a potential superstar in Jimmy Carson and mortgaged the future by giving away their top draft choices. Despite the hype, some of the media were unimpressed.

"Can Gretzky, as great as he is, make the Kings a great hockey team? Don't bet the homestead on it," wrote the Santa Monica *Outlook*.

"Kings Slickered Again By Oilers" read the head on an L.A. *Times* column by Mike Downey.

> "*I kissed that record goodbye a long time ago when Wayne started getting 200 points a year.*"
>
> **GORDIE HOWE**

"Hockey is a game of checkers, not chess pieces," he fumed. "But here is one way to look at Tuesday's trade. The Kings got rooked. To get 'The Franchise,' they gave up the franchise. Leave it to L.A.'s hopeless hockey team to make a trade for the greatest player who ever lived and still get taken."

Jim Murray, the *Times'* legendary columnist, saw it differently: "Listen! Would Caruso want to spend his career singing Gilbert and Sullivan in Leeds? Would Rembrandt want to paint barns? Is Nijinsky going to dance on street corners in Pocatello?

"No. If you know anything about show business, you know you've got to bring the act to Broadway. No matter how good you are in Bridgeport, it's still Bridgeport.

"What made anybody think the greatest hockey player who ever lived was going to stay up there by the North Pole forever?"

The fans were with Murray. They may not have known hockey, but

Point No. 1,851. The NHL gets a new scoring king.

they knew celebrity. In the 24 hours following the trade, the Kings sold 2,500 season tickets. When the season opened, the total had risen to 13,000. Hockey became the hot ticket, 16,005-seat sellouts routine. If there was any doubt, Gretzky settled it himself in his first game. He scored on his first shot. The Detroit goalkeeper he beat was his old Nadrofsky Steelers buddy, Greg Stefan. Before the night was over, he added three more assists. L.A. knew great show biz when it saw it. Move over, Magic Johnson. Move over, Lakers. The Kings were for real.

Compared to creating a winning team, putting the deal together was easy. In the next five years the Kings went through a plane-load of players, two head coaches and one general manager. In each of the first three years they lost the Smythe Division final. In year four they went out in the semi-final. The sellout crowds were still there, but there were grumblings, Gretzky wasn't getting any younger, and the Stanley Cup seemed as far away as ever.

For Gretzky, the points just kept coming. In his first season as a King, he won another Hart Trophy and was named to the second all-star team. In his second, he gave the lie to suggestions made on trade day that he'd never win another scoring title, leading the league in assists (102) and points (142). Along the way, he passed Gordie Howe's all-time NHL point record of 1,850.

"People said we were lucky to get into the final. We had to win Game Five in Calgary and Vancouver and Game Seven in Maple Leaf Gardens. We go into Montreal and win Game One and maybe could have stolen Game Two. We have nothing to be ashamed of."

WAYNE GRETZKY
on losing the 1993 Stanley Cup final in five games to the Montreal Canadiens.

It was no surprise to Howe. "I kissed that record goodbye a long time ago when Wayne started getting 200 points a year."

The next year Gretzky again led the league in points (163) and assists (122). In the fourth season his goal total dropped to 31, but he still led the league in assists with 90. Still, it burned at him. What did his points matter if the Kings kept bowing out early?

The breakthrough came in 1992-93, the season Gretzky thought his whole career might be over. Treatment and rehabilitation of a herniated thoracic disc kept him out of the first 39 games. But once he got into playing shape, he began to roll again with 46 points in his last 27 games. This time the Kings got over the Smythe Division hurdle, won the Campbell Conference crown in a tremendous series with the Toronto Maple Leafs and went into a Stanley Cup final against the Montreal Canadiens that went to a fifth game. Ten minutes after losing that one, a distraught Gretzky, live on *Hockey Night in Canada*, hinted strongly at retirement.

Those who knew him just smiled. Quitting is easy at the end of a season. It gets a lot tougher when the next one starts. The Kings had a new coach in Barry Melrose, a long-haired guru of positive thinking whose unrelenting enthusiasm spread up and down the roster. Gretzky was healthy and hockey once again was pain-free fun. Retire? Not a chance.

In the early years, doubters questioned hockey's staying power. In a town where scenting the hot trend was everything, people wondered if Gretzky had sold Los Angeles on hockey, or on Gretzky? Today, California has three NHL franchises — the Kings, the San Jose Sharks and Disney's Anaheim Mighty Ducks. The Gund brothers, George and Gordon, sold their franchise in Minnesota in exchange for the right to establish one in San Jose for 1991-92. In 1993, Michael Eisner, chairman of the Disney colossus, paid $50 million for rights to put a

Gretzky and the Kings had the 1992-93 Stanley Cup within reach but lost it to the Canadiens in five.

franchise in Anaheim in 1993-94, 50 percent of it going to his old friend, Bruce McNall, for "infringing" on the Kings' territorial rights. (A bit of a hoot, that: McNall was the man who got him interested in establishing a team in the first place.) At the same time, another McNall buddy, Blockbuster Video king H. Wayne Huizenga, leaped in with a second Florida franchise, setting the Panthers up in Fort Lauderdale for an instant rivalry with the Tampa Bay Lightning, who had been in business since 1991.

The face of hockey had changed forever; the game was entrenched coast to coast. And while it truthfully could be said that Bruce McNall's money and Hollywood star-seeking begat the phenomenon, Gretzky was the force that set its roots. "I am convinced that all of these things were triggered by Wayne's impact with us," says McNall.

"And you have to ask yourself: could any other player in the NHL have done it? I don't think there's ever been a player in hockey, maybe in any sport, that could have done what Wayne has done for the Kings and for the game."

"You marvel at how he can hold his level of play so high every night, his intensity level is incredible."

DAVE TAYLOR
L.A. Kings

"I've only been in hockey for a year, so the best I can give you is a fan's perspective," says Eisner. "Wayne had an enormous effect on hockey in southern California because it brought attention to the team, the Kings and to the league – in much the same way Joe Namath did for the American Football League when he came in as a quarterback for the New York Jets back in the beginning of that league."

Californians seem to agree. Silver and black Kings uniforms became an instant hit on the athletic gear market. Their sales records were broken by the Sharks, whose teal, grey, black and white gear with its logo of the shark biting through a hockey stick, outsold almost every professional North American sports

A grateful city's monument to its hero. Wayne Gretzky Day, Edmonton, 1989.

franchise in only their second season. In 1993-94 the Sharks' sales records fell in turn as fans rushed to buy Mighty Ducks gear with its Donald Duck hockey mask logo.

Where will it end? McNall has no idea. "I'm a bit of a dinosaur," he says. "The days of a person owning a franchise are over. When Wayne made his deal with us, players came out of their shells and said, 'Hey, if he can do that, so can we.' It's become simply too big for one person to handle. The Disneys and the Blockbusters and the IDBs [IDB Communications, his new partners in the Kings and in the construction of a new arena in Los Angeles] are the wave of the future. The deal with Wayne changed everything."

Still, he admits, in his wildest dreams he had no idea things would ever become this huge – not for hockey, not for the Kings and certainly not for the marketing phenomenon called Gretzky.

In the ad agency boardrooms it is called "product association factor," or "charisma," or simply "it" – the indefinable, invisible cord that gently but irresistibly pulls the marketplace masses towards products used or endorsed by sports and entertainment heroes. Through the '60s and '70s, it was the all-but-exclusive domain of the TV and movie star. In the '80s, the athletes elbowed their way to the till.

For the handful at the very top, the money made in the games that lifted them to prominence has become a small part of their incomes. When Michael Jordan, the king of the marketing hill, left the Chicago Bulls and basketball in 1993, his estimated earnings for the year were $34 million, with only $7 million coming from the game itself.

The trade – or, as it has come to be known – The Trade – gave the Gretzky market phenomenon a jump-start in California. When the head-and-shoulders best player in a sport ("Admit it, America," blared the cover of the May 1984 *Sport* magazine, "Wayne Gretzky is the best player in any sport.") is abruptly traded by the dynasty he helped create and winds up in Hollywood for dollars then unimagined in his game, the shock waves can't help but hit the advertising nerve centres in places like New York, where hockey has a long history. More difficult to measure, but a factor nonetheless, is the impact of two seemingly inconsequential events a decade apart: The Jersey and The Number.

What if minor hockey had begun at age five when Gretzky first played? There would have been a jersey that fit. No need for Walter Gretzky to tuck in that right side and give a look that set him apart.

"Admit it, America, Wayne Gretzky is the best player in any sport."

SPORT MAGAZINE

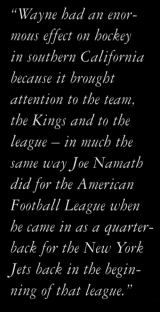

What if, when he got to The Soo and wanted No. 9, Muzz MacPherson had given in, or Brian Gualazzi had said, "Sure, kid. I don't care what number I wear. Take 9."

The point totals wouldn't change. The spot in the Hall of Fame would still be reserved, the place in record book and legend still secure. But would Wayne Gretzky, another No. 9 in the tradition of Howe and Richard and Hull, have the same worldwide off-ice impact if he hadn't been the littlest player with the tucked-in shirt, and then the player with the biggest number of all?

Even the experts cannot define, synthesize or set the parameters of "it." But they know it when they see it, and almost from the beginning they saw it in Wayne Gretzky. "If the world's marketers got together to invent an ideal athlete to endorse products, anyone suggesting an athlete with the credentials and personality of Wayne Gretzky would be accused of pipe-dreaming," wrote *Advertising Age* magazine in 1983.

The ultimate "Wayne's World" – Wayne with Mike Myers and Dana Carvey on Saturday Night Live.

But that was a decade ago. The game has a new crop of stars. The gap between Gretzky and the best of the rest has closed. The league scoring title is no longer his by divine right. There is a "Magnificent One" out there now, a "Next One," a "Golden Brett" and a flood of swift young Swedes and Finns and Russians bringing their own brand of dazzle and flash. Gretzky remains the measuring stick, but in the stretch run of a pro career that, lest we forget, has covered 18 seasons, he faces an ever-growing crowd of challengers.

In a way, they are yet another monument to his impact on his sport. In lifting the game to a new level he pulled a generation of kids with him – kids who worked endless hours on the Gretzky moves, the Gretzky tricks. "When I was a kid, we'd be playing teams and maybe only two or three kids on them could really skate," he says. "Now they're all taking power skating. The records I set in minor hockey won't likely ever be broken. The competition kids face every day is just too strong."

Hockey Night in Hollywood's premiere couple.

Lemieux and Hull have some profile as corporate spokesmen, but only time will tell whether the young guns – Pavel Bure, Alex Mogilny, Jaromir Jagr, Sergei Fedorov and the rest – can woo their share of that marketplace dollar. Lemieux, the heir apparent if his health allows, is already firmly entrenched. Hull, with his cannon shot and blond good looks, is a definite comer. Yet Gretzky has not simply remained on top. At 33, he has become a bigger and stronger marketing tool than ever before.

He's guested on *Arsenio Hall, Good Morning, America* and *The Tonight Show* and was chosen to host *Saturday Night Live.* He's in demand to endorse products far removed from hockey and has his signature line of sneakers, clothing, in-line skates, hockey equipment and electronic games. "A long way from the river," Walter Gretzky used to tease, back when the money and the records were just starting to come. Wally didn't know the half of it. If the Oilers were a rocket to stardom, the Kings were a booster thrust to a whole new level of celebrity which went beyond the dollars that are the usual measuring stick of sport. In Los Angeles he didn't merely build the sport of hockey to what it is now – he transcended it.

THE TUCK

Walter Gretzky wasn't trying to launch a legend. He was just trying to fix it so his six-year-old son could shoot a puck without his stick catching in a hockey jersey four sizes too big.

In those days, minor hockey started when you were 10 and jerseys were ordered accordingly. Who would ever have figured a six-year-old, and a puny, undersized one at that, would need a jersey? The one he got looked like a dress.

Even tucked in, it billowed out at the sides. It looked silly, and when the left-shooting Gretzky followed through, the butt end of the stick would catch in the material. An exasperated Walter finally tucked the side of the jersey deep into the hockey pants. Now the kid looked lopsided, but at least he could shoot.

The tuck-in routine became second nature, then ritual. Strictly speaking, it's no longer necessary. Yet for years now there's been a strip of velcro sewn on the jersey and inside the pants to make certain the tuck stays tucked.

How important is that to the man in the jersey? One of Gretzky's first big endorsement clients was Nike, which also supplied the Edmonton Oilers with their jerseys in exchange for having the Nike logo on the side – the right side. Gretzky's tuck-in was burying the logo. Logic said keep the client happy. Pull out the jersey. No way. The jersey stayed tucked. Nike provided the Oilers with a new set of unies. The logo was now on the left side.

There was, however, one big game when the jersey was worn normally: the 1978-79 WHA all-star game. He was a skinny 17-year-old donning an all-star jersey that was far too wide. As usual, he reached down and started to tuck in the right side. A big hand appeared and pulled it back out. It was Gordie Howe.

"Gimme that thing," he said. From somewhere the greatest legend in professional hockey produced a needle and thread and sewed a tuck in each side of the jersey to give it a proper fit.

Gretzky would have preferred to tuck it in the way he always did. He didn't say a word. Who argues with Gordie Howe?

EXCALIBUR

Gretzky used and endorsed a Titan stick for almost a decade. Unlike most of the game's big shooters with their deeply curved blades and buggywhip shafts, he had always preferred a moderate curve and a shaft that was as rigid as possible.

That rigidity made the stick extra heavy – a real concession for a player who trimmed his equipment, from pads to gloves, of every spare ounce. But now the Easton people were making aluminum sticks; so they set out to produce one with the characteristics Gretzky wanted, but lighter. Once they found a shaft he liked, they worked on the curve of the blade. Now they had the consistency, the configuration, the stiffness with less weight.

Meanwhile, they worked on special gloves. If he was going to endorse Easton sticks, they wanted him to be wearing Easton gloves. Again, he was particular: softer leather in the palm, the cuff cut back, the wraparound at the top of the glove taken off to allow for easier wrist flexion.

Wayne was satisfied. The gloves were fine, the stick was great. They began talking contract. That was where Barnett came in.

"The aluminum shafts

they'd been using had a dull finish," he says. "Twenty rows up, or on TV, you couldn't tell whether they were aluminum or wood. We wanted something that would make people realize that he hadn't just changed brands, he'd changed product. We wanted something that would be special for both parties."

Easton explored ways to polish the aluminum. They never quite got it to Barnett's liking. "I want something that looks like it

came from Tiffany's," he said.

Easton came back with a stick buffed at high speed with the type of polish used at trophy shops.

"He'll never use this," said president Jim Easton.

"It's perfect," said Barnett.

Gretzky took it into action. When the camera lights hit it, it shone like a beacon, and *Hockey Night in Canada* commentator Harry Neale reached back to Arthurian legend for a fitting description. "Gretzky," he said, "has a new Excalibur."

Ultra-Wheels

CHARISMA

In the early 1980s when he was a teen sensation in sports, there were Gretzky wristwatches, bedspreads, clocks, mirrors, lunch kits, wallpaper and a 50-card Gretzky collection years before the trading-card craze.

If Gretzky liked it, Michael Barnett, his friend, long-time agent and now president of International Management Group's hockey division, okayed it, and there was a guarantee that product and marketing would be strictly first-class.

Product association factor. Charisma. "It." Call it what you will, Gretzky has it. The years have taken the nervous kid of the "I grew up in GwGs" of the early commercials and turned him into the polished, well-dressed businessman/athlete speaking about the virtues of companies and products such as Coca-Cola, Domino's Pizza, Easton, Harleybrands, L.A. Gear, Sharp Electronics, SLM, Thrifty Car Rental, Ultra-Wheels, Upper Deck and Zurich Canada.

The trick of it, says Barnett, is not to sit back and wait for the prospective endorsements to walk in the door. The trick is to go looking for clients armed with a concept of how an athlete's name can best be used to heighten the profile or sales of the client's products.

"Wise athletes don't endorse products they don't use," Barnett says. "Conversely, they shouldn't stop using a product just because they don't endorse it. For instance, Wayne uses a particular line of skates because he likes them, because they work well for him. But we've never been able to come to terms on a contract. We could have an endorsement tomorrow if he was willing to switch skates. But that would be a business decision. And the hockey decisions supersede them. Always."

L.A. Gear

Sharp Electronics

SLM

Coca-Cola Future Stars
Hockey Camp

Domino's Pizza

Harleybrands

Thrifty Car Rental

Easton Sports

Coca-Cola Ltd.

"The trade to L.A. kick-started the hockey card craze in the U.S., lifting it near the top of the multi-million dollar sports memorabilia market. Wayne Gretzky's rookie card is without a doubt the most prized possession in collections across the continent, and around the world."

ALEX KLENMAN
columnist, Canadian Sports Card Collector

Practice makes perfect. Bill Tuele of the Oilers kept this early example of Wayne perfecting his autograph technique.

Fan mail favourite: the occasional letter without an address didn't keep the post office from delivering Wayne's continuous stream of fan mail.

The King of Ice Hockey
Wayne Greatsky
Try Brantford (Home Town) Canada

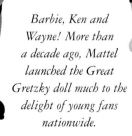

Barbie, Ken and Wayne! More than a decade ago, Mattel launched the Great Gretzky doll much to the delight of young fans nationwide.

Shades of Saturday Night Fever. *Wayne's early '80s fan club kit.*

Fundraising extraordinaire: from 1980 to 1992, Wayne hosted a celebrity tennis, then baseball tournament, raising $1,000,000 for the Canadian National Institute for the Blind.

White House salutations: President Clinton congratulates Wayne on being honoured by the Big Brothers of Los Angeles.

Truly one of a kind – Wayne's daughter Paulina owns this one and only authentic signed Topps card.

THE WHITE HOUSE
WASHINGTON

February 1, 1994

Mr. Wayne Gretzky
Los Angeles, California

Dear Wayne:

I am delighted to extend congratulations as you are honored by Big Brothers of Greater Los Angeles. Your tremendous accomplishments on the ice and your generous community service have made you a positive role model for young people everywhere and a personal hero for the youth of Los Angeles.

Best wishes for continued success.

Sincerely,

Bill Clinton

Stylish homecooking at the hottest spot in town: Wayne Gretzky's. Call (416) 979-PUCK.

This Honus Wagner card found a new home with Gretzky and McNall for the tidy sum of $450,000 U.S.

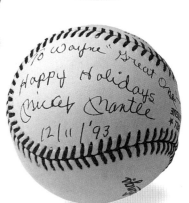

Drysdale, Koufax, Rose and Mantle pass on their best to the Great One.

SUPERAGENT

Michael Barnett's association with Wayne Gretzky was built on the understanding that for Wayne to be the best player he could be, Michael had to be the best agent he could be.

For some it's difficult to think of one man without the other. Were the friendship not rock-solid, Barnett might easily develop a complex.

On November 12, 1982, *Sports Illustrated* told Barnett that Wayne had been selected as its Sportsman of the Year, but if word got out any earlier than three days before the announcement in their year-end issue, they would switch to their second choice. Meanwhile, they had to get a photo session with Wayne without anyone in the

media catching on.

The magazine flew a man into Edmonton to study Northlands Coliseum, and then rented it for the night of November 29. The film crew flew in, waited until the Coliseum closed, blacked out the boards and set up the cameras and lights. They had everything but Wayne who was flying home from Detroit.

Solution? Barnett was about Wayne's size and colouring. They sneaked him into the rink at 3 a.m., dressed him in Wayne's uniform and took about a

million shots. Then they removed every trace of their visit, returned to New York, picked the two best pictures, rented the Coliseum in secret again, returned, positioned Gretzky precisely where Barnett had been and took the cover shot of No. 99 stretched out on the ice with his reflection making it a double image.

Barnett-as-Gretzky surfaced once more. The Gretzky wedding was set for July 16, 1988 in Edmonton. TV crews swarmed over St. Joseph's

Cathedral-Basilica to make certain the lighting would be right. And what better way to test it than to film another wedding first? And guess who was getting married in that same church on April 2? Michael Barnett and Dalyce Giordano.

"I didn't mind them filming it," Barnett says. "But they kept calling it The Rehearsal!"

Above: *"A great business manager and a great friend."* Gretzky and Michael Barnett with the 1989 Hart Trophy.

130

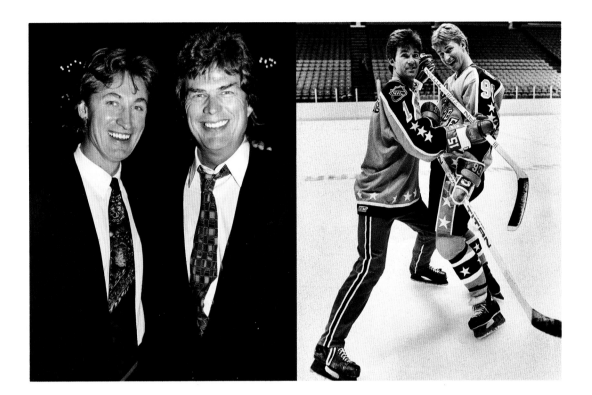

THE CANADIAN CONNECTION

The minister began his sermon: "In the beginning, there was Walter. He did cometh unto Brantford, where he and Phyllis begat Wayne, and the prophets said, 'He shall become king of Kings …'"

Alan Thicke, TV sitcom star and self-confessed hockey groupie from Kirkland Lake, Ontario, was doing his shtick, the act he'd performed at so many Wayne Gretzky celebrity tournaments and NHL award events.

"For it was written that a Great One shall be born unto Canada in a manger. And his name shall be Gretzky, and he shall be known as Wayne Diet Coke Domino's Pizza Upper Deck Easton Ultra Wheels Air Canada Breakfast of Champions Sharp Tiny Handicam the First …"

Thicke's accompanist at this 1994 Big Brothers banquet honouring Wayne Gretzky as the *Athlete of the Decade* was the award-winning composer-arranger David Foster from Victoria, British Columbia. The three Canadians had hit it off from the beginning.

"The first big test," says Thicke, "was when I was divorced and cancelled on the same day. Later, when he was ending a relationship, I had to do it for him and we both did it for David."

Seeing the success of Gretzky's tennis and later softball tournaments, Foster formed the David Foster Foundation and staged an annual ball tournament and dinner of his own in Victoria to raise money for organ transplants for children.

Thicke was inches away from Gretzky minutes after the final-game loss to the Montreal Canadiens in the 1993 Stanley Cup final. "I put my arm around him and said something. He wouldn't even look at me. He muttered a curse word and stepped through the curtain to do the TV interview where he announced his possible retirement.

"My jaw dropped. I wanted to shove my arm through the curtain, grab him and say, 'Schmuck! You won't feel this way later.' And, of course, he didn't."

Above left: *Gretzky and Foster.* Above right: *Thicke and Gretzky.*

ELVIS LIVES

As manager of rock star Bryan Adams, Bruce Allen is no stranger to celebrity. Because Wayne Gretzky is a huge Bryan Adams fan and a frequent backstage guest at concerts, Allen has seen the two interact.

"They're very comfortable in each other's presence. ... When people come in, Wayne says, 'Hi, I'm the bass player.'

"Every guy in music wishes he were an athlete. Every athlete wishes he were in music. Wayne has watched Bryan come up, and Wayne was much bigger at the start. Adams didn't become a star until 1985. They're exactly the same age. And there's something else. Canadians notoriously pull down people who make it. But the Canadian public to this day love Adams and love Gretzky. They don't care whether he plays for L.A. or where he plays."

So where does Gretzky sit in the entertainment firmament?

"If you want to put it in rock terms," Allen says, "there are rock stars and rock stars, and then there is Elvis Presley. Wayne is Elvis."

Above: *Gretzky and Adams backstage at Madison Square Garden during Adams'* Into the Fire *tour, summer 1987.*

STARDUST

Bruce McNall can remember to the day when he knew that his $15-million deal for Wayne Gretzky had bought him more than an athletic superstar.

"It was a couple of days after we'd made the deal. I had to go to a big cocktail party, just stop in for a couple of minutes, and then we'd go out for dinner. Wayne said he'd wait in the car; he didn't belong at a thing like that.

"But I coax him, because I'm not going to be that long. We're standing in the doorway, and there are about 200 people in there, including about every star and big hitter you could name. Wayne was uncomfortable, just being there.

"But we go in, and in a couple of minutes, we get separated. When I look back, the first thing I see is this long, long line of Hollywood heavies. They're all waiting to get Wayne's autograph."

Not a Kings game goes by without a strong Hollywood contingent in the stands. Goldie Hawn and Kurt Russell are hockey fanatics. Mary Hart, Michael J. Fox, James Woods, André Agassi and Candice Bergen have all made the trek to the Great Western Forum.

Tom Hanks was there two days after winning his Academy Award. There is no doubt that the catalyst has been Gretzky.

But why? Along with everything else, McNall contends, "a bit of an aura of mystery. Magic Johnson may be more fascinating, more recognizable. But Wayne's not really out there. There's this little wall, a sense of privacy. Now he's entering the era of legend."

Michael Barnett tends to agree. "He's been asked to be a presenter at the Acad-emy Awards. He's been asked to present something on about every show that presents anything. If he was an American who'd become the hockey star he is while living in L.A., he wouldn't be as endeared to the people here as he is now. But he's a foreigner, a star who's chosen to come here. It sets him apart."

Above: A pair of L.A. aces: Gretzky and Lakers basketball legend Magic Johnson.

EIGHTEEN FIFTY-ONE

On January 26, 1961, the day Wayne Gretzky was born, Gordie Howe scored his 467th NHL goal. By the time Gretzky entered the league in 1979, Howe's lead stood at 786-0. In points, he was ahead by a tidy 1,809.

He had one more NHL year left in him in Hartford, and was still good enough to add 15 goals and 26 assists to his career totals.

As he piled up the scoring titles and blew away the point records, it became apparent that, barring injury, Wayne would inevitably pluck the two career marks that had seemed unassailable: Howe's 1,850 points and

801 goals. It was simply a question of when it would happen.

Fittingly, the point mark fell in Edmonton on October 15, 1989 where so many of them had been recorded. It came on a game-tying goal with 53 seconds left in regulation time – on a backhand. Immediately, the game was put on hold as Howe, who had followed the team for days in antici-

pation of the big event, came out to take part in ceremonies honouring the NHL's new point king.

The superstitious would tell you it was fated to happen. Trivia buffs have the details of Gretzky's first-ever NHL goal committed to memory: Scored on October 14, 1979 against the Vancouver Canucks and goalie Glen Hanlon with Vancouver's Stan Smyl

in the penalty box. Gretzky tries to shoot, half fans on the puck, and it dribbles through Hanlon's legs. But look at the time – it was scored in the third period: 18:51.

Above: *The official NHL 1,851-point scoresheet.*
Facing page: *Gretzky celebrates his overtime goal that beat the Oilers the night he broke Howe's point record.*

October 15, 1989: The NHL point record falls at last. This page: *Gordie Howe, Janet and Walter offer congratulations.* Facing page: *Steve Duschesne and Dave Taylor drew assists on the goal that gave Gretzky 1,851 points and Gretzky added the finishing touch with the winning goal in overtime as the Kings beat the Oilers in Edmonton.*

*"My first choice is to do it in Los Angeles. If I can't,
I'd like to do it in Edmonton."*

WAYNE GRETZKY

*"I would prefer to have him do it here. He lived ten years here. The city meant a lot to him.
Hockey is what's important. I can't believe him. He always does it in such a dramatic way."*

WALTER GRETZKY

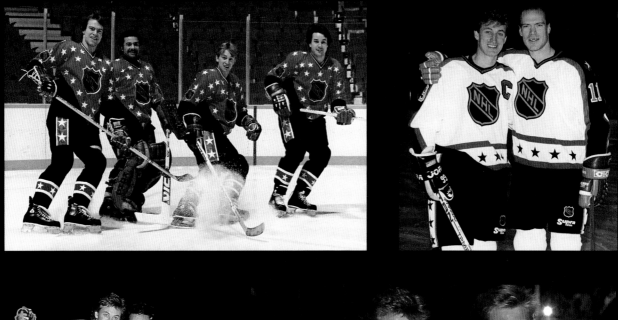

Above left: *Gretzky was never the only Oiler to wear the jersey of the Campbell Conference All-Stars.*
For the 1982 game in Landover, Maryland, Mark Messier, Grant Fuhr, Gretzky and
Paul Coffey were can't-miss choices. Above right: *Gretzky with Mark Messier,*
reunited as teammates for the 1989 All-Star game in Edmonton.

Below: *1993 and perennial All-Stars:*
Gretzky with Paul Coffey (left), and Brett Hull (right).

The All-Star Collection –
Wayne's 1994 All-Star jersey.

Wayne Gretzky has been named the first team all-star centre in eight seasons
and the second team centre in five others. He has scored more all-star game
goals (12) than any player and holds the record for most goals (4)
and most points (4) in a single period – all recorded
in the third period of the 1983 all-star game.

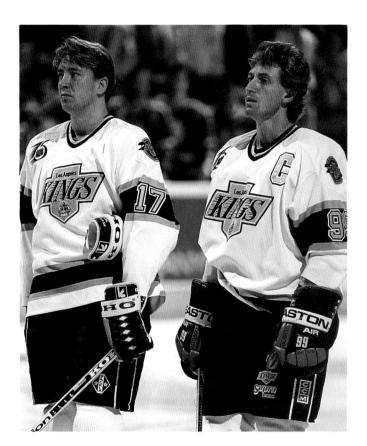

THE RIGHT WING FINN

When they unveil Jari Kurri's portrait in the Hockey Hall of Fame, as inevitably they will, it should go to the immediate right of the Wayne Gretzky portrait. That's where he was for eight glorious years with the Edmonton Oilers – on the right wing of a line that read Kurri, Gretzky and Whoever.

The Oilers looked everywhere for a left-winger who could play their style: Blair MacDonald, Dave Semenko, Brett Callighen, Raimo Summanen, Esa Tikkanen, Mike Krushelnyski. On the right there was Kurri. Period.

He came to the Oilers for their second NHL season from his native Finland. Sather promptly tried the 20-year-old Finn with the 19-year-old Gretzky. "The first game I am with him, I get three goals," says Kurri.

"I think to myself, 'Hmmm. This could be good.'"

It wasn't good. It was great – so great that he's spent most of his career answering the same old question: "What is it with you two guys? Magic? Telepathy? What?"

"It's just about styles," he shrugs. "The way we play the game and the way we see the game, it's the same. Wayne sees it so much better, so much faster than anyone else. When we were in Edmonton, I was a

shooter. I was able to get to the hole for him, and he was always able to find me. It's just as simple as that."

Gretzky, he says, can see things happening before they happen. "With Wayne, you can't look at a hole and think, 'There's no use going for it because there'd be no time or no way he can get the puck to me.' You have to hit the hole as soon as you see it start to open, because he'll have seen it before you do, and the puck will be there

when you get there. And when he doesn't read the game, he reads me. We've done it for so long now, he just knows where I'm going to go."

Gretzky proclaims, "Jari's such a complete hockey player. If we ever told him just to go out and check the other team's top players, he'd put them in his pocket."

Above: *Kurri and Gretzky – reunited as Kings.*

THE BOOK ON 99

Almost always, there has been the myth: Gretzky never gets hit. "It's like trying to hit confetti," Glen Sather said in the early years. Later, fans whose teams he'd just destroyed would snarl, "The league says don't hit him. They don't want their big star out of games. Besides, he's always had Semenko or McSorley. You hit Wayne, they hit you."

Barry Melrose used to believe the myth. Then he became head coach of the Kings, and rapidly altered his thinking.

"He rarely gets really drilled," he concedes. "But he gets hit more here than he used to because, more and more, he puts himself in the traffic areas, which he has to do for this team. In Edmonton, and here in the first couple of years when we had lots of scoring talent, he could afford to play the perimeter and get his points. But the way we are now, the way we play, he has to get into those traffic areas and as a result, he gets bounced around a lot more."

"He's almost created his own monster," says assistant coach Cap Raeder, who was in Los Angeles when Gretzky arrived. "He's gotten so many points over the years, that's how people see him. When he came off his back injury and wasn't get-ting the points, he was playing some of the best two-way hockey ever. But the media and the fans aren't looking at that. They expect points."

As coaches, they've seen Gretzky under every condition. And yes, he does have down games. "You can tell right away when he's on," Melrose says. "He's got the step, the fire, the antic-ipation. He's yapping the referees, he's on the guys on the other team. When he's not on his game, he's more laid back, more complacent on the bench. Mind you, in a down game he may chip in three assists. And when you think about it, it's amazing that he isn't down more often. The pressure on him is unbelievable, because if he doesn't get those three points, people think he's had a bad game."

Above: Gretzky on the receiving end of a punishing check.

DISC JOCKEYS

"We weren't trying to get Wayne Gretzky back to the point where he could play hockey again," says Dr. Ronald Kvitne. "The first objective was to get him to the point where he could have a normal life. If he could play hockey, that would be a bonus."

Technically, the injury that kept Gretzky out of 39 games in the 1992-93 season was the herniation of a thoracic disc. The deteriorating disc material was pinching the nerves down the right side of the chest. The pain made it impossible for Gretzky even to consider starting the season. When he called the press conference to announce that he would sit out training camp, take treatment and hope things improved, there was a better-than-even chance

that he was saying goodbye to the game forever.

"It's really remarkable how he came back," says Dr. Kvitne, the Kings doctor and a physician with L.A.'s famous Kerlan-Jobe Clinic. "For an average person on the street in a non-athletic profession, it would be a devastating injury, and that person probably wouldn't make it back to a normal activity level. For someone in a contact sport, the odds against returning were much higher."

The first decision was the big one: surgery, or exercise and treatment. Surgery would almost certainly mean the end of the hockey career. "We were calling around the world for the most experienced people in the field," says Kvitne. "Some said surgery, some not. Finally, it was decided to stick with exercise and treatment. And you've seen the results."

The results were Gretzky's return to hockey for the last 45 games of the season to

lead the Kings into the playoffs and clear to the Stanley Cup final.

The final, non-medical summation was left to Gretzky. "I've figured a way I can play forever," he joked. "Play 45-game seasons. But you know the best part? I can bend over and pick up my kids again."

Above: Gretzky's injuries in the '91 Canada Cup final, a foreshadowing of the back problem that nearly ended his career in 1993.

ROLE MODEL

They almost lost Wally three years ago. He had finally retired and was up a ladder painting when the big headache hit. He'd suffered a brain aneurysm. Delicate surgery was required.

For a while, they didn't think he'd make it. But he did, and he's battling back with all the old determination.

Sometimes, as is common in such cases, the short-term recall plays tricks. But ask him about the kids and the games and the trips in the Blue Goose. Ask him about the Stanley Cups and the records and the thousands of hours out there on "Wally Coliseum." It is all there, as fresh and golden as ever.

For Walter the unsought perks that went with being the father of Wayne never changed a single thing that mattered.

He was Walter Gretzky. He worked at Bell Canada, servicing teletypes and other communications equipment. If you asked him how his son was doing, he'd probably say, "Which one?"

From the time Wayne turned pro there was never a need for Walter to work. He had ulcers and a perpetual ringing in his ears caused by an accident in the old telephone-pole-climbing days. He seldom got to sleep before 3 a.m. and rarely did a day go by without a headache. Once Wayne convinced him to quit. He took a six-month leave of absence to try it out. On decision day, he reported for work as usual at 8 a.m.

"All my life I've taught the kids to stick to things, to give it their best," he said. "What kind of an example would I be, laying around at home living off my pension and Wayne's money?"

As much as possible, Walter didn't let his son's celebrity make any difference at home. Certainly one thing never changed. The phone still went nuts. In the minor hockey days there had been the hundreds of calls made all over southern Ontario, arranging the games and the ice times and the tournaments. Now it was Wayne, calling collect from wherever his team happened to be.

"I work at the Bell," Wally said. "They give me my cheque, and I give it right back to them."

Above: *Walter and Phyllis in the family trophy room.*

143

THE GRETZKY LINEUP

What the tabloids could never fathom – as they accused Janet Jones Gretzky of wooing away Canada's national hockey treasure by promising him Hollywood stardom – was that this was a love story that happened to happen just when Bruce McNall was pulling the biggest trade in the history of professional hockey and maybe of professional sport.

She was blonde and beautiful and had made movies and appeared in *Playboy*. She was Hollywood, and she – not McNall and his millions, not Peter Pocklington, who wanted the cash – was the one who was taking Gretzky away. "I didn't understand it at the beginning, being in a fishbowl like that," she says. "But we were so much in love, nothing bothered us. We were just … wow!"

Now there are three more reasons to wow – Paulina and Ty and Trevor. "I think Paulina is one of the luckiest little girls in the world," Janet says, "because she's going to have a great relationship with her father, a male image in her life. What's funny is that she has no interest in hockey at all. She just loves her father for what he is, because she doesn't really grasp what it's all about nor does she care."

But, since hockey does play such a huge part in the family environment, it seemed reasonable to ask Janet for a scouting report on the children.

"Paulina … she was older than a 10-month-old baby. It was in her face, in her little scowl. She's got a lot of wisdom. I call her my little old lady. She sits there with this little round face and her little mouth and her glasses. She's got a lazy eye that will

be corrected later, but right now the glasses seem to fit her personality. I think one day she's going to take off her glasses, let her hair down and be a princess.

"I really enjoy my days talking to her. Paulina will take love any time you want to give it to her. Ty and Trevor want affection when they want it. Otherwise, they're busy. Paulina is always there for me. Kids will always put you through

a lot and I'm ready for that. But I can see in her heart she's never going to want to hurt me.

"Ty and Trevor are opposites. I'd say Ty is Wayne and Trevor is Marty McSorley. Ty needs a lot of attention because he's very sensitive. He gets a lot of it, especially from the hockey players. He has a natural athletic ability to pick up sports very easily. It's whether he's going to apply it, or whether he wants to.

"Trevor is one bowl of grit. He loves to cuddle, but he'll punch you in the face at the same time. I think they're going to be very close. The best thing that's happened to Ty if he's going to be an athlete is Trevor, because Trev is going to kick him in the butt.

"Ty just wants to play, and Wayne will never push him into it. I'll probably be more pushy than Wayne, because I like them to be competitive. Being Wayne Gretzky's kid might open some doors, but you've still got to get in there and prove it."

Janet still wants to have at least one more child, but not before putting her full effort into the career she put on hold. She is working on an album with the support of award-winning producer and song-writer David Foster. ("We're not just doing this," Foster says. "Janet is good. She is going to surprise a lot of people.")

"I've always had the passion to do it," she says, "but two years ago I put my nose to the grindstone and went for it."

Above: *The Gretzky hat trick: Paulina, Ty and Trevor.*

THE GRAND MASTER

Gretzky has always been a source of fascination for Russian coaches. Viktor Tikhonov, legendary coach of the Soviet national hockey team and his predecessor, Anatoli Tarasov, were bitter off-ice enemies, but they agreed on Gretzky. Tarasov: "He is the only player who can play the game above ice level. He sees it from 100 feet above." Tikhonov: "He sees things from up above. He sees things before they happen. If he was playing chess, he would be a grand master."

Tikhonov tried to sum up Gretzky for the Soviet press. "When he gets the puck behind an opponent's net, whether he is at even strength or a man short, the spot behind the net becomes a special rink built only for him, because no one else can do back there the things he can. It is almost as though the entire game is being transferred from every other part of the ice to that place. And then it becomes a new game, and Gretzky invented it."

CHAPTER SIX

99 ON 99

There
is a Varadi Avenue

look to the big house in Beverly Hills as Wayne Gretzky sits down by the pool to contemplate past and future: kids and noise in all directions, and everyone crowded into the kitchen. The main part of the house is still in recovery mode after extensive earthquake damage. Sheets of plastic hang floor to ceiling. The air reeks of plaster dust and paint. There are more people than chairs in the kitchen.

Facing page: *In Los Angeles, Gretzky gives Ty a little help with his wardrobe, a shot to be added to an album of his own as the family tradition continues.* Above: *The precious family photo album from Varadi Avenue.*

Janet, Walter, Phyllis and four drop-ins sit as the opportunities arise. At least one of the three phone lines is ringing at any given moment. The kids have friends over to swim, raising the decibel count past jackhammer.

"Just like home," he grins. "Just like home."

The guessing game has already started as to what the future holds for No. 99. He's got three years left on his new four-year contract, which averages out to $8.25 million a year, and says he'd like to play at least that long, proving he can continue to perform at his own elevated standard. He will not linger to become known as a good third-line centre. He is not the first to say he'll know when it's time to leave, but few have said it with such utter conviction.

But what then? What fills the holes left by practices he no longer has to attend and the rough-and-ready fellowship of the dressing room, which no outsider can ever truly comprehend or join? Will he ever hear a national anthem without pining for

those moments at centre ice with the butterflies fluttering and the adrenaline pumping and the hands twitching on the stick?

What's out there that can possibly match lifting a Stanley Cup or a Canada Cup and skating a victory lap with the sweat dripping from your face and the crowd roaring tribute to you and the teammates with whom you've gone to war and won? What happens when you no longer hear: "Los Angeles goal … his 35th of the season … by No. 99 – W-AY-NE GRETZ-KY!"

"When I quit, I just want to walk away from it."

The words are Wayne's, spoken in 1983 for the epilogue to his father's book, *Gretzky: From the Back Yard Rink to the Stanley Cup*. He was 22, approaching the full flush of his awesome talents. But he had already been in the pressure cooker for most of his life. When he looked past hockey, it was to an undefined something in a world where the spotlight would finally click off.

Now, five days before he would become the NHL's all-time greatest goal

scorer, he remembers saying those words and how right they seemed at the time. But …

"This is my 17th year in pro," he says. "But Barry Melrose was the one who said, 'No, it's not. It's really 30 years of hockey. And he's right. I started when I was three, so my life has been hockey for 30 years. So to finish hockey and go and do something else, to go to work in an office or whatever, I don't see myself doing that. It's not my style, not my life."

What, then?

"I don't want to coach. That's out. I don't think I'd have the patience to be a good coach. I don't think the things that I do could translate verbally. And I have enough trouble getting myself ready for a game, let alone 20 other guys. It takes all my energy. I feel sorry for coaches. They have to have a special quality, and I don't have it.

"As for being a general manager, I could never do that. The best GMs are the ones who are the most honest. They have to be able to call a guy in and say, 'You know, you might prove me wrong one day. You might be better than I think. But right now you're not good enough to make my team. I'm sending you to the minors.' Or call a guy in when they know he's just bought a house and got the kids settled in school and his wife has just begun to make new friends and say, 'Maybe I'm making a mistake, but we've just traded you. Good luck.'

"I couldn't do that to anybody, and to be a good GM you have to. Consequently, neither of those positions is open to me."

> *"This is my 17th year in pro. But Barry Melrose was the one who said, 'No, it's not. It's really 30 years of hockey. And he's right. I started when I was three, so my life has been hockey for 30 years."*
>
> **WAYNE GRETZKY**

Countless rinks, countless
practices, in good times and
bad, Walter was always
there to lend a hand or ease a
moment. Wayne has a theory
about his dad's recovery from
a brain aneurysm: "I think s
God's way of saying, 'This i
a good man. Better keep him
down here a while longer.'"

*Practice is more than skating, passing and shooting. It is the dressing room banter, the laughter
exchanged in the moments between drills performed a thousand times and more,
and the work is never over until the last media question has been answered.*

Ownership, then. People have been projecting him as an owner since the money started getting enormous as his career entered its final stages. "He wants to be a builder," says Michael Barnett. "He'll relish the challenge of either taking a new team or a team with problems and getting right down to work. He has such a clear and precise vision of what it takes to build a winner that the only way to implement it will be to sit in the ownership chair."

"It's a Lego thing to him," adds Bruce McNall. "And he's got definite ideas of where the pieces fit."

Gretzky isn't anywhere near that certain.

"If Bruce offered me a chance to be involved with his team at an ownership level, then I would do it, as a helper, maybe, or an advisor. But somewhere else? Listen, people see the end result. It's easy now, with us selling out and San Jose and Anaheim selling out, to say, 'Yeah, hockey's great. We knew it could go here in California.' But six years ago it was a lot of blood, sweat and hard work. Every single day, June, July and August, running from TV show to radio show to magazine interview to newspaper, trying to push and promote the sport.

Six years ago we started rebuilding from the ground up, and I feel good that I was a part of that. But I don't want to be anywhere else. This is where I like to be. This is where I want to stay."

He is running out of tomorrows, and knows it. But he has learned to treasure the todays. "When you're young," he says, "you think you appreciate the great things in your life, but you really don't. I appreciated winning all the championships

"So I go to the rink happy and I leave it happy, and when the young guys ask me how come I'm always so perky I tell them hey, we're being paid to play this game. Enjoy it, because some day it will be gone."

WAYNE GRETZKY

and awards when they were happening, but I really think I appreciate the game more now than I did when I was 23. Not that I took it for granted, but when it was over I'd know we played again tomorrow. At the end of every season I could say, 'Okay, guys, see you in September.' But how many Septembers are there left?

"Nobody has to tell me that I'm down to the last strokes here. I may have three good years left in me, maybe only two. That's where I'm at now. So I go to the rink happy and I leave it happy, and when the young guys ask me how come I'm always so perky I tell them hey, we're being paid to play this game. Enjoy it, because some day it will be gone."

"What has it been like, being Wayne Gretzky?" he is asked. The question catches him by surprise. He rolls it around in his mind, sorting the sections of 30 years. One by one, he brings them out for examination.

THE EDMONTON YEARS "I don't want to sound arrogant about my career, but it was so easy in the early years. There were games where my dad would say, 'Well, you didn't play very well,' and he was right. But I could play badly on that team and get five points. Easily! Say we had four power plays and I had a goal and an assist. Then a couple of regular assists and maybe a shorthanded point, and that was five points – playing poorly.

"It's one of the reasons I think my records will stand for a long time: I just don't think, particularly with expansion, that any player coming in will be fortunate enough to be surrounded by that much talent, maybe more talent than any one team has ever had, and all so young that we could stay together a long time.

*For Ty Gretzky, some practice days are special: the days he gets to go work with his dad,
suit up with the Kings in their dressing room and, in the moments before or after the workout,
get in some practice of his own with the other No. 99. For Wayne, the drive home with
Michael Barnett is the bridge between hockey and business.*

"Think about this: no team had ever scored 400 goals or more in a season. We did it five straight years, and nobody's done it since. I was in the perfect spot with the perfect team."

THE L.A. YEARS "One day about a month ago, Barry kept us in the dressing room for an hour after practice, just talking about the way things were going, which wasn't very well. He didn't do it as a punishment, he did it to try to get it across to the young players how lucky they were to be playing here.

"'You leave the rink here and nobody knows who you are,' he said. 'You can lose three in a row, go out to a restaurant, you go have a beer, nobody bothers you. You play in Montreal or Toronto or Boston and when you've lost three in a row, you don't go anywhere but straight home, because if you go to a bar or a restaurant or down to the corner for a paper, there'll be people there telling you you stink. Here, you can go wherever you want and get away.'

"He was right. The kids don't realize how fortunate they are. Guys who come to this team who've played in those other places understand the pressures those teams are under to perform. Maybe we'd be better off if the young guys came here after being somewhere else. People are big sports fans here. They come around. They talk to you. But there's not that constant, day-to-day pressure. Here, the only pressure is whatever you put on yourself."

SCHOOL "When I was in school, the one thing I truly resented was that for me there was no in-between. The teachers either spoiled me rotten or were really hard on me, and all I ever wanted was to be treated like a, quote unquote, normal student.

"I can't imagine Paulina or Ty going to school in Canada. That's not a slap. I love Canada. But hockey is so big there, such a huge part of everybody's life. They'd be Wayne Gretzky's kids, like Kim was Wayne Gretzky's sister. I'd be worried for them every day: Are they being treated fairly? How are the other kids to them? How are the

other parents to them? How are the teachers treating them? Here, my kids aren't the only ones whose parents are celebrities. They can have a normal school life."

FATHERHOOD "When I was 23 I never thought about having kids. I felt like I was the kid, the son of my mom and dad, and my responsibility was to them. I didn't ever think, 'Well, in the next few years I'm going to have three kids.' It never entered my mind. Then, overnight, I'm thirty-three. Your priorities change. Your thoughts change.

"When I was 23, I could wake up in the morning and say, 'I'm going to Toronto today, tomorrow I fly to Florida. I fly here to work, I drive there to work, I can go to this charity event.' I just kind of went, non-stop, and I loved it.

"Now, the first thing I think is my daughter's in school until June, which gives us a couple of months after that to do things, and then she's back in school in September, and Ty will be, too. I've got to go there and do this. Now how do I fix it so Janet and the kids can go with me?

"And I want to do that. It's a priority. Paul Anka told me that the greatest thing he ever did as a parent was have his kids around him all the time. If he travelled, they were there. If they wanted to bring friends, he brought them along, too. The kids weren't deprived of their friends, but they were able to do things as a family and everybody loved it. 'I could afford it, so I did it,' he said. 'You can afford it. Do it.' So I can see it coming: the Gretzky Family Road Trip."

"When I was 23 I never thought about having kids. I felt like I was the kid, the son of my mom and dad, and my responsibility was to them. I didn't ever think, 'Well, in the next few years I'm going to have three kids.'"

WAYNE GRETZKY

*A day in the life of the Gretzkys begins with breakfast
with the kids and some television time with Trevor.
Then, everyone's off and running.*

"The joy that you get from the love of your kids — when my daughter and my sons get up in the morning and come in and give me a hug and a kiss and say, 'Daddy, I love you,' there's nothing that can match it."

WAYNE GRETZKY

"I make sure that never a day goes by when I am not eternally thankful for the good health that my children enjoy."

JANET JONES GRETZKY

For two people in spotlight-bathed careers, "alone" is a word in the dictionary. It makes the quiet times all the more precious.

"Define being a dad," he is asked. There is a long silence. Then: "The joy that you get from the love of your kids. When my daughter and my sons get up in the morning and come in and give me a hug and a kiss and say, 'Daddy, I love you,' there's nothing that can match it."

FAMILY DISCIPLINE "I'm such a softie. When the kids misbehave we give them a Time Out, which is like going to the penalty box, only it's to their room or into the house if we're outside. But I'm not very good at it, because when Paulina presses her nose against the window and looks out at me with those big eyes …

"There are family rules, sure, but the only one I'm strict about is that they can't watch TV in my room. I tell them I'll watch it with them anywhere else, or we'll watch videos, whatever. But when Daddy goes to his room, he's resting. He's getting ready to go to work. It's my place for peace and quiet."

THE FOLKS "People wonder sometimes when they hear me call my dad 'Wally' or my mom 'Phyllis.' Actually, it started from a TV commercial for a detergent called Big Wally. Brent saw it, and when Dad came into the room he yelled, 'Here's Big Wally!'

"It wasn't disrespectful. With my parents, respect for other people was everything, and if we didn't show it to someone we heard about it right then. This was a joke, and it just stuck. And if Dad was Wally, then Mom had to be Phyllis. She did draw the line, though, when Brent came out with 'Big Wally and Silly Philly!'

"There's no end to the autographing. At the rink, at home, in my office while we talk business — he just sits in front of a table of stuff and signs his way through it. Next day, the table's full again."

MICHAEL BARNETT

"My mom sacrificed more than all of us together. She never talked about it, but it's true. When I was nine years old, I can remember her bugging Wally about needing new curtains. 'Forty dollars, Wally,' she kept saying. 'I need $40 for curtains.' For two weeks my dad never really answered. He just kept saying, 'I'll take care of it, Phyllis. I'll take care of it.'

"The thing was, it was August, and I needed new skates. They cost $35, and money was tight. One day, without saying anything to Mom, he took me down and bought me the skates, only on the way home he said, 'Don't tell your mom just yet.' I couldn't figure that out. But when we got home he went straight to the closet and got two bedsheets. He was hanging them over the windows when my mom came into the room. Dad didn't miss a beat.

"'See, Phyl,' he said. 'Everybody's happy. Wayne's got his skates, and you've got your curtains.'

"Big Wally. I miss him in so many ways. Going for the goal record, even when I wasn't really close to it he'd have been around, talking about the games, telling me if I played well, or badly. Like the old days.

"The brain aneurysm was a very near thing. We almost lost him. But he's getting better every day. It's just amazing. He's quit smoking, he sleeps better, he looks healthier, all the stress is gone. The way he was living, he was headed for destruction, a heart attack or something. Now he'll probably live 20 years longer than he would have. You know, everything happens for a reason. I think it's God's way of saying, 'This is a good man. Better keep him down here a while longer.'

"It's funny, the perception of my dad in the dressing room. He's a hard-nosed, blue collar, eight-to-five guy. You know, Canadians grew up that way. So when one of the young guys comes to practice saying he can't skate today because he's got a cold or his ankle is sore, one of the vets like Marty or Charlie will look up and say, 'What would Big Wally say about that, Wayne?'

"I tell them exactly what he'd say. He'd say, 'A cold? Get your ass out on the ice!' What usually happens then is, the guy goes back out onto the ice.

"The money really doesn't mean all that much. I put it in trust funds for the kids. But the greatest thing I can do with it is when I can buy something for my dad.

"I remember one time I bought him a boat. I can still see him at the kitchen table, phoning everybody in Brantford and saying, 'Can you imagine what this dummy did? He bought me a boat.' But he was so proud.

"He's helping coach some little guys in Brantford now. I asked him how it was going and he said, 'I don't mean to be rude, but these kids are a lot better than you were at that age. More of them know how to handle the puck. When you played, only one or two of them could.'

"You know what's nice? You look at them now, after all these years, and they're still holding hands, always touching each other somehow — scratching each other's back, things like that. They fell

in love forever, and nothing can change it. All those years, and they're still the happiest couple I know."

It's almost dinner time in the mansion in Beverly Hills. The kids are still running and yelling, the workmen still pounding, the phones still ringing, the kitchen still jammed. In 18 hours, the Kings face a must-win game with the San Jose Sharks and then back home to face the Vancouver Canucks — two important divisional games with not only a playoff position at stake, but Wayne's pursuit of the NHL 802 goal record now just two goals away. Until then, this is his universe.

"Just like home," he says again.

"You know, it's all relative. Obviously, my house is bigger than my folks' house ever was. But my dad's front door was always open and there were always people coming through. Next-door neighbours, people just dropping in. In the winter time, kids in the backyard playing hockey. Our house was like Grand Central Station. Janet grew up that way, too. And now we're the adults and the kids are our kids and their friends. It's like only the faces have changed."

Wayne Gretzky gets up and heads poolside to hug a tiny, soaking, precious chunk of his future. Hand in hand, they walk up the stairs to the kitchen.

A friend pokes Walter Gretzky in the ribs. "Long way from the river, Wally," he says.

"Not that far, really," he says. "Not that far."

> *"Obviously, my house is bigger than my folks' house ever was. But my dad's front door was always open and there were always people coming through ... and now we're the adults and the kids are our kids and their friends. It's like only the faces have changed."*
>
> **WAYNE GRETZKY**

KOHO CHAMPION HOOK

APRIL 10, 1974, *Minor Hockey/Turkstra Lumber:*
1,000th goal against Waterford, assisted by Terry St. Amand.

SHER-WOOD 500 99

FEBRUARY 3, 1978, *Junior A/Soo Greyhounds: 138th point, the OHA record for most*
points by a rookie, vs. the London Knights – two goals and two assists recorded with this stick.

JANUARY 2, 4, 5, 1979, *WHA/All-Star Team:*
Wayne's autographed stick from fellow WHA All-Stars.

TITAN First NHL Goal

OCTOBER 14, 1979, *NHL/Edmonton Oilers: first NHL goal, scored at 18:51 of the third*
period vs. the Vancouver Canucks, assisted by Brett Callighan and Blair McDonald.

TPM2020 TITAN

OCTOBER 15, 1989, *NHL/Los Angeles Kings: 1,851 points – the NHL record for most points –*
scored at 19:07 of the third period vs. the Edmonton Oilers, assisted by Steve Duschesne and Dave Taylor.

EASTO

MARCH 23, 1994, *NHL/Los Angeles Kings: 802 goals – the NHL record for most goals –*
scored at 14:47 of the second period vs. Vancouver Canucks, assisted by Luc Robitaille and Marty McSorley.

THIS STICK IS NUMBER 043 USED
BY WAYNE GRETZKY ON THE
NIGHT HE BECAME HOCKEY'S
ALL-TIME LEADING SCORER, OCTOBER 15, 1989

...da Davis Oct 15/89   Wayne Gretzky 99

802 goal puck.

802
*Wednesday, March 23, 1994.
Los Angeles Kings vs. Vancouver
Canucks. 14:47 of the second
period on a Kings power play.*

"*Robitaille with
Gretzky the trailer –
gives it to Gretzky.
Right side to McSorley
– back in front to
Gretzky ... he scores!
Wayne Gretzky's
NHL record book is
now complete. He's
the all-time leader
in points, assists and
now, with his 802nd
goal, the all-time lead-
ing goal scorer in the
history of the National
Hockey League!*"

BOB MILLER
TV Play-by-Play Announcer,
Prime Ticket

"*More than any previous record, the historical significance of 802 really
hit home with me when the game was halted after the goal.
It made having my wife, my children and my parents there even more special.*"

WAYNE GRETZKY

*"To me, it's the greatest game in the world and I feel
fortunate to be able to play in the NHL."*

WAYNE GRETZKY

It began on the farm
by the river, watching
Hockey Night in Canada
on Saturdays, dressing
for church on Sundays
and living on the ice
every free moment.
It will end, as it must,
when the time is right.
But for Wayne Gretzky,
the game is still there to
be played, the Stanley Cup
still there to be won.
And he wouldn't have it
any other way.

A small boy in a black and silver hockey jersey with GRETZKY 99 on the back, blond hair peeking out beneath his helmet, works his way down the ice in the Great Western Forum, his father skating backwards in front of him, handicam whirring.

Ty Gretzky doesn't know his father is famous, or even what famous means. All he knows is that hockey is a fun game, and his father plays it with the big people, the way he does with his friends.

In some ways, it may not be easy being Ty Gretzky, learning to skate and playing minor hockey in California. Already, people want his picture, especially if it's with his dad. Sometimes it takes a long time to get past them just to get to the car.

But his dad will be there, helping him and playing with him and making sure it stays a fun thing he does because he loves it. And there will be winter vacations, when he and Dad will drive to the farm through the snow in a car that's bound to be called the Goose. They'll skate on the Nith, and play hockey and laugh, and drink hot chocolate at the kitchen table while his dad rubs his toes to make the cold go away.

He is three years old, and the adventure has just begun.

CAREER RECORD

SEASON		CLUB	LEAGUE	REGULAR SEASON					PLAYOFFS				
				GP	G	A	PTS	PIM	GP	G	A	PTS	PIM
1976-77		Peterborough	OHA	3	0	3	3	0	—	—	—	—	—
1977-78	ab	Sault Ste Marie	OHA	64	70	112	182	14	13	6	20	26	0
1978-79		Indianapolis	WHA	8	3	3	6	0	—	—	—	—	—
	cd	Edmonton	WHA	72	43	61	104	19	13	10*	10	20*	2
1979-80	efg	Edmonton	NHL	79	51	86*	137*	21	3	2	1	3	0
1980-81	ehijk	Edmonton	NHL	80	55	109*	164*	28	9	7	14	21	4
1981-82	ehijklm	Edmonton	NHL	80	92*	120*	212*	26	5	5	7	12	8
1982-83	ehijmnoq	Edmonton	NHL	80	71*	125*	196*	59	16	12	26*	38*	4
1983-84	ehimq	Edmonton	NHL	74	87*	118*	205*	39	19	13	22*	35*	12
1984-85	ehijmnopqr	Edmonton	NHL	80	73	135*	208*	52	18	17	30*	47*	4
1985-86	ehijkr	Edmonton	NHL	80	52	163*	215*	46	10	8	11	19	2
1986-87	ehimqr	Edmonton	NHL	79	62*	121*	183*	28	21	5	29*	34*	6
1987-88	gnp	Edmonton	NHL	64	40	109*	149	24	19	12	31*	43*	16
1988-89	eg	Los Angeles	NHL	78	54	114	168	26	11	5	17	22	0
1989-90	gi	Los Angeles	NHL	73	40	102*	142*	42	7	3	7	10	0
1990-91	fhijk	Los Angeles	NHL	78	41	122*	163*	16	12	4	11	15	2
1991-92	f	Los Angeles	NHL	74	31	90*	121	34	6	2	5	7	2
1992-93		Los Angeles	NHL	45	16	49	65	6	24	15*	25*	40*	4
1993-94	fgi	Los Angeles	NHL	81	38	92*	130*	20	—	—	—	—	—
NHL Totals				1125	803	1655	2458	467	180	110	236	346	64
WHA Totals				80	46	64	110	19	13	10	10	20	2
Professional Totals				1205	849	1719	2568	486	193	125	246	366	66

* Led league
a OHA Second Team All-Star (1978)
b Named OHA's Rookie of the Year (1978)
c WHA Second Team All-Star (1979)
d Named WHA's Rookie of the Year (1979)
e Won Hart Trophy (1980, 1981, 1982, 1983, 1984, 1985, 1986, 1987, 1989)
f Won Lady Byng Trophy (1980, 1991, 1992, 1994)
g NHL Second Team All-Star (1980, 1988, 1989, 1990, 1994)
h NHL First Team All-Star (1981, 1982, 1983, 1984, 1985, 1986, 1987, 1991)
i Won Art Ross Trophy (1981, 1982, 1983, 1984, 1985, 1986, 1987, 1990, 1991, 1994)

j NHL record for assists in regular season (1981, 1982, 1983, 1985, 1986, 1991)
k NHL record for points in regular season (1981, 1982, 1986, 1991)
l NHL record for goals in regular season (1982)
m Won Lester B. Pearson Award (1982, 1983, 1984, 1985, 1987)
n NHL record for assists in one playoff year (1983, 1985, 1988)
o NHL record for points in one playoff year (1983, 1985)
p Won Conn Smythe Trophy (1985, 1988)
q Won Emery Edge Award (1983, 1984, 1985, 1987)
r Selected Chrysler-Dodge/NHL Performer of the Year (1985, 1986, 1987)

NATIONAL HOCKEY LEAGUE RECORDS HELD OR SHARED

CAREER

1. Most Goals: 803 – 15 seasons (1979-1994), 1125 games
2. Most Assists: 1655 – 15 seasons (1979-1994), 1125 games
3. Highest Assist Per Game Average (min. 300 assists):
   1.471 – 1655 assists in 1125 games
4. Most Points: 2458 – 15 seasons (1979-1994), 1125 games (803 goals, 1655 assists)
5. Highest Points Per Game Average (min. 500 points):
   2.185 – 2458 points in 1125 games (1979 - 1994)
6. Most Goals by a Centre: 803 – 15 seasons
7. Most Assists by a Centre: 1655 – 15 seasons
8. Most Points by a Centre: 2458 – 15 seasons
9. Most Overtime Assists: 12 – 15 seasons
10. Most Goals, Including Playoffs: 913 – 803 regular season and 110 playoff goals
11. Most Assists, Including Playoffs: 1891 – 1655 regular season and 236 playoff assists
12. Most Points, Including Playoffs: 2804 – 2458 regular season and 346 playoff points
13. Most Games Scoring Three-or-More Goals: 49 – 15 seasons (36 three-goal games, 9 four-goal games and 4 five-goal games)
14. Most 40-or-More-Goal Seasons: 12 – 1979-80 to 1990-91
15. Most Consecutive 40-or-More-Goal Seasons: 12 – 1979-80 to 1990-91
16. Most 50-or-More-Goal Seasons: (tied) 9 in 15 seasons
17. Most 60-or-More-Goal Seasons: (tied) 5 in 15 seasons
18. Most Consecutive 60-or-More-Goal Seasons: 4 – 1981-82 to 1984-85
19. Most 100-or-More-Point Seasons: 14 – 1979-80 to 1991-92, and 1993-94
20. Most Consecutive 100-or-More-Point Seasons: 13 – 1979-80 to 1991-92

SINGLE SEASON

21. Most Goals: 92 – 1981-82, 80-game schedule
22. Most Assists: 163 – 1985-86, 80-game schedule
23. Most Points: 215 – 1985-86, 80-game schedule
24. Most Games Scoring at Least Three Goals: 10 (done twice) – 1981-82 (6 three-goal games, 3 four-goal games, 1 five-goal game); 1983-84 (6 three-goal games, 4 four-goal games)
25. Highest Goals-Per-Game Average: 1.18 – 1983-84, 87 goals in 74 games
26. Highest Assists-Per-Game Average: 2.04 – 1985-86, 163 assists in 80 games
27. Highest Points-Per-Game Average: 2.77 – 1983-84, 205 points in 74 games
28. Most Goals, Including Playoffs: 100 – 1983-84, 87 goals in 74 regular-season games and 13 goals in 19 playoff games
29. Most Assists, Including Playoffs: 174 – 1985-86, 163 assists in 80 regular-season games and 11 assists in 10 playoff games
30. Most Points, Including Playoffs: 255 – 1984-85, 208 points in 80 regular-season games and 47 points in 18 playoff games
31. Most Goals by a Centre: 92 – 1981-82, 80-game schedule
32. Most Assists by a Centre: 163 – 1985-86, 80-game schedule
33. Most Points by a Centre: 215 – 1985-86, 80-game schedule
34. Most Goals, 50 Games from Start of Season: 61 – 1981-82 (Oct. 7, 1981 to Jan. 22, 1982, 80-game schedule); 1983-84 (Oct. 5, 1983 to Jan. 25, 1984, 80-game schedule)
35. Longest Consecutive Point-Scoring Streak From Start of Season: 51 games – 1983-84, 61 goals, 92 assists (streak ended by the Los Angeles Kings and goalie Markus Mattsson, Jan. 28, 1984)
36. Longest Consecutive Point-Scoring Streak: 51 games – 1983-84, 61 goals, 92 assists (Oct. 5, 1983 to Jan. 28, 1984)
37. Longest Consecutive Assist-Scoring Streak: 23 games – 1990-91, 48 assists

38. Most Assists: (tied) 7 (done three times) – Feb. 15, 1980 at Edmonton
    (Edmonton 8, Washington 2); Dec. 11, 1985 at Chicago (Edmonton 12,
    Chicago 8); Feb. 14, 1986 at Edmonton (Edmonton 8, Quebec 2)
39. Most Assists, Road Game: (tied) 7 – Dec. 11, 1985 at Chicago
    (Edmonton 12, Chicago 8)
40. Most Assists by a Player in His First NHL Season: 7 – Feb. 15, 1980
    at Edmonton (Edmonton 8, Washington 2)
41. Most Goals, One Period: (tied) 4 – Feb. 18, 1981 at Edmonton, third
    period (Edmonton 9, St. Louis 2)

PLAYOFFS – CAREER

42. Most Points: 346 – 110 goals, 236 assists
43. Most Goals: 110
44. Most Game-Winning Goals: 21
45. Most Three-or-More-Goal Games: 8
    (2 four-goal games and 6 three-goal games)
46. Most Assists: 236

SINGLE PLAYOFF YEAR

47. Most Points: 47 – 1985, 17 goals, 30 assists in 18 games
48. Most Short-Handed Goals: (tied) 3 – 1983 (twice vs. Winnipeg in
    division semi-finals, won by Edmonton 3-0; once vs. Calgary in
    division finals, won by Edmonton 4-1)
49. Most Assists: 31 – 1988 (19 games)

SINGLE SERIES

50. Most Points in Final Series: 13 – 1988, 3 goals, 10 assists
    (4 games plus suspended game vs. Boston)
51. Most Assists in Final Series: 10 – 1988
    (4 games plus suspended game vs. Boston)
52. Most Assists in One Series (other than final):
    (tied) 14 – 1985 conference finals (6 games vs. Chicago)

SINGLE PLAYOFF GAME

53. Most Short-Handed Goals: (tied) 2 – April 6, 1983 at Edmonton
    (Edmonton 6, Winnipeg 3)
54. Most Assists: (tied) 6 – April 9, 1987 at Edmonton
    (Edmonton 13, Los Angeles 3)
55. Most Points, One Period: (tied) 4 – April 12, 1987 at Los Angeles,
    third period, 1 goal, 3 assists (Edmonton 6, Los Angeles 3)
56. Most Assists, One Period: (tied) 3 (done five times)

ALL-STAR GAMES – CAREER RECORDS

57. Most Goals: 12 (14 games played)
58. Most Points: (tied) 19 (14 games played)

ALL-STAR GAMES – GAME RECORDS

59. Most Goals: (tied) 4 – Campbell Conference 1983
60. Most Goals, One Period: 4 – Campbell Conference, third period, 1983
61. Most Points, One Period: 4 – Campbell Conference, third period,
    1983 (4 goals)

NATIONAL HOCKEY LEAGUE AWARDS

Hart Memorial Trophy (Regular Season Most Valuable Player)
1980, 1981, 1982, 1983, 1984, 1985, 1986, 1987, 1989
Art Ross Trophy (Regular Season Scoring Championship)
1981, 1982, 1983, 1984, 1985, 1986, 1987, 1990, 1991, 1994
Conn Smythe Trophy (Stanley Cup Playoffs Most Valuable Player)
1985, 1988
Lester B. Pearson Award (NHL's Outstanding Player – Selected by Players)
1982, 1983, 1984, 1985, 1987
Lady Byng Memorial Trophy (Most Gentlemanly Player)
1980, 1991, 1992, 1994
Emery Edge Award (Best Plus-Minus Rating)
1983, 1984, 1985, 1987
Chrysler-Dodge/NHL Performer of the Year
1985, 1986, 1987

NATIONAL HOCKEY LEAGUE – ALL-TIME SCORING LEADERS

GOALS

	Teams	GP	Goals
1. Wayne Gretzky	Edmonton, Los Angeles	1125	803
2. Gordie Howe	Detroit, Hartford	1767	801
3. Marcel Dionne	Detroit, Los Angeles, New York Rangers	1348	731
4. Phil Esposito	Chicago, Boston, New York Rangers	1282	717
5. Mike Gartner	Washington, Minnesota, New York Rangers, Toronto	1170	617
6. Bobby Hull	Chicago, Winnipeg, Hartford	1063	610

ASSISTS

	Teams	GP	Assists
1. Wayne Gretzky	Edmonton, Los Angeles	1125	1655
2. Gordie Howe	Detroit, Hartford	1767	1049
3. Marcel Dionne	Detroit, Los Angeles, New York Rangers	1348	1040

POINTS

	Teams	GP	Points
1. Wayne Gretzky	Edmonton, Los Angeles	1125	2458
2. Gordie Howe	Detroit, Hartford	1767	1850
3. Marcel Dionne	Detroit, Los Angeles, New York Rangers	1348	1771

Statistical Appendix compiled by the Los Angeles Kings.

*All-Star lineup: Gretzky with four of the NHL
all-time scoring leaders – (left to right) Jean Béliveau,
Bobby Hull, Gordie Howe and Phil Esposito.*

OPUS PRODUCTIONS INC.

President/Creative Director: Derik Murray
Designer: Dave Mason/Dave Mason & Associates
Design/Production Assistant: Pamela Lee
Artifact Photography Producer: Andreanne Ricard
Artifact Photography: Derik Murray Photography/
Perry Danforth, Grant Waddell, Jason Stroud,
with the assistance of Kathryn Hollinrake,
Virginia MacDonald and Malene Plum Johansen

Vice President, Sales and Marketing: Glenn McPherson
Marketing Coordinator: David Attard

Vice President/Publishing Director: Marthe Love
Author: Jim Taylor
Editor: Audrey Grescoe
Assistant Editor: Jennifer Love
Production Manager: Paula Guise
Editorial Coordinator: Wendy Darling
Research Consultant: Phil Pritchard, HHoF
Visual Coordinator: Colette Aubin
Assistant Visual Coordinator: Cathy Love
Project Accountant: Kim Steele
Administrative Assistant: Robin Evans

Opus Productions would like to thank the following:

International Management Group: Michael Barnett,
Susan Felts, Jamie Fitzpatrick
Wayne Gretzky's, Toronto: Robert Ross and Staff
Bitove Corporation: Nick Bitove, Tom Bitove
Mackay + Wong Design: Gord Mackay
Hockey Hall of Fame: Scotty Morrison,
A. David M. Taylor, Jeff Denomme, Phil Pritchard,
Craig Campbell, Andrew Bergant
Sports Illustrated: Karen Carpenter, Jeff Weig

*Opus Productions would like to extend a special thank you to the Gretzky family, especially Wayne, Janet, Walter, Phyllis and Kim,
in appreciation of their cooperation and support; and Paulina, Ty and Trevor for their patience and enthusiasm.*

Opus Productions would like to acknowledge the following for their assistance and support:
KODAK CANADA INC. – all artifacts photographed exclusively on Ektachrome Professional film.
FEDERAL EXPRESS CANADA LTD. – all express delivery shipments worldwide.
Booth Photographic Ltd. – Printfile Archival Preservers
This book is printed on Lustro gloss 100 lb. text manufactured by S.D. Warren.

Bruce Allen, Randy Berswick, Kimberly Blake, Bruce Allen Talent ■ Murray Angus ■ Mike Anscombe, CHCH TV ■
Rob Apatoff, Stacey Flemming, LA Gear ■ Bryant Avery, Joan Coombs, *Edmonton Journal* ■ Gary Bartlett, *Edmonton Sun* ■ Bert Bell ■
Tom Best, HarperCollins ■ Jim Bishop, TGL Sales Ltd. ■ Bob Borgen, *Prime Ticket* ■ Maurice Bridge, Peter Ladner, *Business in Vancouver* ■ Michael Burch,
Nick Rundall, Whitecap Books ■ George D. Burke, David L. Thomas, Bull, Housser & Tupper ■ Greg Chamandy, Harleybrands Inc. ■ Roark Critchlow ■
David Csumrik ■ Ken Derrett, Labatt Breweries ■ Bennie Ercolani, National Hockey League ■ Carmen Garcia, McNall Sports and Entertainment ■
Jack Grushcow ■ Rob Hindley, Chris Jordan, Bettina Scargall, Coca-Cola Ltd. ■ Guy Hockin ■ Dan Infanti, Christine Olijnyk, Sharp Electronics ■
Ron Kerr, Thrifty Canada Ltd. ■ Alex Klenman ■ Lionel Koffler, Firefly Books ■ Aggie Kukulowicz ■ Janet Lindsay, Tony Luppino, Zurich Insurance ■
William J. Livingston, The Lovero Group ■ Heather MacAuley, Royal York Hotel ■ Rick Minch, Nick Salata, Los Angeles Kings ■
Sandy Mitchell, Polaroid Canada ■ Sue Parker Munn ■ Susan Niles, Ultra-Wheels ■ Joeannea Parker ■ Bronwen Pencarrick ■
Cliff Pickles ■ Larry Regan, National Hockey Alumni ■ Peter Scarth, Kodak Canada ■ Terry St. Amand ■ Deborah Winser ■

ARTIFACT CREDITS

Opus Productions would like to thank the following individuals and institutions for their generous assistance in allowing access to their artifacts and memorabilia:
Michael Barnett ■ Brian Cooper ■ Bill Comrie ■ John Czarny ■ Alan Frew ■ Murray Fried ■ The Gretzky Family ■ John Groezinger ■ Hockey card selection
courtesy of Gary Gagen, Let's Collect … ■ Hockey Hall of Fame ■ Wayne Kooyman ■ Travis McPherson ■ National Hockey League ■ Rick Scheffler ■
Barry Snetsinger, Copps Coliseum ■ Ron St. Amand ■ Jim Taylor ■ Bill Tuele, Edmonton Oilers ■ John Utley ■ *Wayne Gretzky's*, Toronto ■ Temple Wright ■

SELECT BIBLIOGRAPHY

Edmonton Oilers. *Official Guides*, 1980 through 1987. ■ Los Angeles Kings. *Media Guides*, 1988 through 1993. ■ Dinger, Ralph, and Duplacey, James, eds. *The National Hockey League Official Guide & Record Book, 1993-94*. Montreal: National Hockey League, 1993. ■ Downey, Mike. "Kings Slickered again by Oilers". *Los Angeles Times*. August 10, 1988. ■ Durslag, Melvin. "L.A. may not be the place for a guy like Gretzky". *The Herald Examiner*. Los Angeles, August 12, 1988. ■ Gretzky, Walter, and Taylor, Jim. *Gretzky: From the Back Yard Rink to the Stanley Cup*. New York: Avon Books, 1984. Toronto: McClelland and Stewart, 1984. ■ Murray, Jim. "He'll bring L.A. out of ice age". *Los Angeles Times*. August 11, 1988. ■ Reilly, Rick, and Gretzky, Wayne. *Gretzky: An Autobiography*. Toronto: HarperCollins, 1990. ■ Safarik, Alan, and Reimer, Dolores. *Quotations on the Great One*. Vancouver: Arsenal Pulp Press, 1992. ■ Waldner, Mike. "What can he do for Kings?" *The Outlook*. Santa Monica, August 10, 1988. ■ Whyte, Kenneth. "Nobody's Fifteen Feet Tall". *Saturday Night*. January/February, 1990. ■

Opus Productions would like to thank the following individuals who contributed their time in the form of interviews for the purposes of this book, January – May, 1994:
Tony Acone, Gus Badali, Michael Barnett, Ted Beare, Tom Best, Kurt Browning, Don Cherry, Brian Cooper, Michael Eisner, David Foster, Janet Gretzky,
Kim Gretzky, Phyllis Gretzky, Walter Gretzky, Wayne Gretzky, Arthur Griffiths, Dr. Euclid Herie, Bob Hockin, Gordie Howe, Charlie Huddy, Ron Kerr,
Randy Kitchen, Aggie Kukulowicz, Jari Kurri, Dr. Ronald Kvitne, Ron Low, Kevin Lowe, Mary McCoy, Matt McCoy, Bill McIntosh, Bruce McNall,
Muzz MacPherson, Marty McSorley, Dick Martin, Barry Melrose, Mark Messier, Eddie Mio, Scotty Morrison, Cap Raeder, Mary Rizzetto, Rick Rizzetto,
Sylvano Rizzetto, Rick Rizzo, Nelson Skalbania, Gordon Smeaton, Barry Snetsinger, Greg Stefan, Bob Taylor, Alan Thicke, Bill Tuele, Vladislav Tretiak.